DISCOVER YOI
THROUGH THE

Gospel of John

A *Renew* Six Step Study

Rachael Shalloe-Cooper

malcolm down
PUBLISHING

Contents

Foreword

"Every scholar of the Scriptures, who is instructed in the ways of heaven's kingdom realm, is like a wealthy home owner with his house filled with treasures both new and old. And he knows how and when to bring them out to show others."

This little parable of Jesus from Matthew 13 sums up Rachael's book for me.

Not that Rachael is a wealthy home-owner, although she does run a business that manages properties. And she probably wouldn't claim to be a scholar either. But she really has been instructed in the ways of heaven's kingdom realm and Discover Yourself Through the Gospel of John is like a storehouse of treasure that Rachael opens up for us.

When I first came across Rachael's Six-Step-Study it was an event only open to women. I had to sneak a look on YouTube to see what it was all about. I watched, fascinated, as she explained these steps and then walked through a passage of scripture using the them. It was like being at a spiritual gym – a thorough workout of holy stretches, impact, weights, distance and of course some ways to find a resting heartbeat. I've also met some of those who have joined in this process with Rachael week by week and seen the effect it has had in their own lives and faith.

Rachael helps lead one of our churches and I had wondered how she had managed to grow from a new Christian to a mature, resilient and wise leader. This is the Holy Grail of church leadership: good discipleship. Over the years at Rising Brook, we've hosted many conferences, seminars, and workshops from some leading discipling practitioners, and I am involved in a number of church and ministry organisations nationally and internationally where real life-changing spiritual growth is recognised as the most important factor in fruitful mission. So, what is it that has enabled Rachael to become the open, honest and insightful person we read about in this book?

I think that Rachael truly understands the need to be nourished by the Word of God – to eat the book, as God encouraged Ezekiel. And she also knows the need to drink from the fountain of life and be filled with the Holy Spirit. This book is all about understanding the Word of God and inviting the Holy Spirit to use it as a light so that its power and grace are applied to ordinary and everyday life.

And it also helpfully sees discipleship like we might see a gym, music and sports development or joyfully learning new skills. Discipleship is training; and training requires coaching, patience, resilience and rewards. Training also means that we grow in wisdom, stature and favour – able to live well and win the prize. I think this is what Rachael has given herself to, which means she's now got this solid, attractive and powerful faith. It makes me want to invest in my own spiritual training more wholeheartedly.

The structure that Rachael outlines is very thorough. The idea is to bring ourselves to the bible and allow its truth to impact our own lives – thoughtfully, prayerfully and intentionally. When we are honest about who we are and how we think, then this devotional handles the bible in such a way that we can seize these thoughts and feelings, interrogate them and bring God's truth and grace into the reality of our everyday, up-and-down, tidy-and-messy, good-and-not-so-good lives.

There are some great titles. Rachael has found some stunning perspectives in the stories and teaching in John's gospel. I was struck by the idea of being 'captured' in the story of Jesus' arrest, and how I handle being captured, and how I might invite God to release me.

There are some great questions. These are the kind of questions to really dig into and they make you re-read scripture and re-read your heart. "Can you think of a time when you were on the receiving end of someone else's frustration?" Mmm, let me see . . . can I? This is real and relevant stuff – certainly not a boring old textbook.

There are some great stories. Rachael invites us with openness and honesty into her own life. Her honesty helps me trust her and the revelation of God she brings from her own knowledge and experience of the love of Jesus. This is one of the reasons I really enjoy being on a team with Rachael. She's got a great sense of humour and manages to see both the funny and serious sides to life.

So, if you're wondering how to do business the Jesus way, or handle regret from the past, or find faith to walk with friends, or have hope for your marriage and family, then use this guide to take you through John's story of Jesus. Try the Six Steps structure to become more self-aware, Bible aware and Holy Spirit aware. And see what treasures there are in here – some old, some new – that will bring the Kingdom of Heaven close to your heart.

Martin Young
Rising Brook Church
January 2020

Introduction

Renew is a group led by two ladies, Rachael and Hayley. Friends since childhood, Rachael and Hayley found themselves struggling with areas of their lives and wanted to study with like-minded ladies to discover what God wanted them to apply to their lives from the Bible. From there came the Six Step Study. This six-step study is a technique developed that aims to see the world changed by the Word of God. We believe that the Word of God is life-giving to everyone and that you don't have to be a scholar to allow the Bible to impact your life. Jesus wants to be a part of every aspect of our lives and no matter what questions we have about the life ahead of us, the answer is in the Bible. It doesn't need to be complicated; God's Word is the answer. By studying these six steps on a weekly basis over the course of this devotional, we pray that your life will be completely transformed, and that you will be fully alive.

We developed this study to help us overcome our many personal challenges of life, whether that be motherhood, marriage, work, church, friendships or ministry. Time and time again we went back to the Bible with these simple six steps to depict what God wanted to say to us about these issues and find answers from Jesus Himself.

As we continued this journey it was evident to the people around us that our perspectives were shifting and our lives were different. When probed as to what this could relate to, we shared the six-step study. We then went on to use it in a weekly study at our church and again the steps in this study began to show fruit in the lives of the ladies who were using it.

Since developing the group studies, we have been asked to share the methods behind it and show people how this will work. This devotional will show you who Jesus is, who you are in Him and how He guides us through our lives every day.

You won't need to spend long in this study; in just an hour or so a week you will begin to see your life transformed through allowing the Holy Spirit to lead you.

We believe that study is better together. So, if you would like to see live video studies and meet like-minded ladies, you can find our group on Facebook by searching for Renew Six Step Studies or visit our website Renewstudies.com.

Our prayer for you is this:

Father, we thank You for each person that is about to start this study. We thank You for the life-giving words that You've given to us to share. We thank You that Your Word never changes and never fails. We pray that as each person works through this study, they will receive fresh revelation of who they are, how much they are loved, and how unique they are. We pray, Lord, that they see the desire in Your heart for their life and that seed becomes something that grows into full bloom as they embark on this journey of discovery.

In Jesus' name, amen.

How to Use This Study

This study is solely focused on journaling and discovering how God is speaking to us and the impact of applying these changes to our lives. If you don't already have a nice shiny new journal, I advise you to get one just for this process. It's a great tool to use and also really useful to look back on to see how much life is changing. With any goal in life we need to measure our success and keeping track of our spiritual growth is a wonderful thing to do.

Step 1 – Remove

Before reading the weekly devotions take some time to journal the things that are on your mind. Don't worry about the content of what you are writing, just use this time to clear your mind in order to allow God to speak to you during your devotional time. What you write can be good or bad, there are no rules here, just let your thoughts flow on to the paper. Once you feel you have finished clearing your mind read the portion of scripture highlighted for that week. Then go on to read the devotional for that week.

Step 2 – Reflect

Throughout the devotions there will be questions in bold; use these questions to reflect on the portion of scripture you have read and what you feel God might be saying to you that week.

Take your journal and write down anything that stands out to you or words that God is placing in your heart.

Step 3 – Relate

Take a look at what you wrote in the last two steps. Can you see anything relating together? For example, you may have written in your 'Remove' an issue you are facing at work or church, then in the 'Reflect' section you may have written that God is speaking to you about sharing your feelings more or overcoming fear, if you see anything contrasting write it down.

Step 4 – Replace

In that last step you have been looking for contrasting thoughts, a lie versus the truth. If you found one, which you will have if you're looking hard enough, ask God, 'What would you like me to replace this with?' Write it down.

Step 5 – Respond

This is the accountability part. Ask God, 'What three steps, spiritual or practical, can I put into place over this coming week to aim towards affirming Your truth in my life?' Write them down.

Step 6 – Renewed

This step is to take into the week with you. Take a little bit of time at the end of each day and assess how you have done with the steps God gave you. Have you noticed any differences?

Why Do I Exist?

WEEK 1

Read John 1:1-18

The book of John is such a beautiful joy to read. Although it's hard for me to pick a favourite chapter, I have to say John 1 is near the top of the list. I like to read The Passion Translation. I know some say it's a paraphrase and not a like-for-like translation but I'm not reading it to educate myself historically; my main reason for reading the Word is to develop my relationship with Jesus, and I think that the words in this translation are a perfect way for me to identify His splendour. My heart leaps with each word I read when looking over these verses!

The first 18 verses of John are said to have been the words of a hymn or poem written and cherished by first-century believers. I can see why they were cherished too – what beauty we see in just reading over the words.

Let us begin with verses 1 and 2: we learn that in the very beginning Jesus was already there. *He was with God yet fully God, together – face-to-face, in the very beginning.* I can't even begin to imagine how beautiful that was. It brings me great joy to visualise this picture. Can you picture the fun that they had with creation? I become very childlike when I think about the plan that went into creating a me! I find myself pondering the whole discussion around who Rachael might be, what she might look like, what she will sound like, the strands of DNA code that go in to her make-up, what she will do, who she will meet and what her lifetime will include.

Our creation is far beyond our comprehension, but we begin to see the depth to who we are as individuals; it's not our own ego anymore as we ponder our make-up because we can see the care and detail that went into creating us. With this in mind I find that I'm able to be much kinder to myself and I actually begin to dream a little bit more. Try it for yourself, ponder this question:

How might the Father and Son have discussed your creation?

In verse 3 we discover that through the creative inspiration of Jesus all things were made. The Passion Translation says, *'For nothing has existence apart from Him!'* Let us ponder that for a moment.

We have *no* existence apart from Jesus! Without Him we simply don't exist. That's powerful. Can you imagine not existing? The dictionary describes non-existence as a fact or state of not existing or not being real or present, so if we don't exist with Jesus, we become non-existent. We live a life that's not real or fully present, one that is false and not aligned to the purpose we were designed intentionally for.

This makes me think back to creation; before God created the heavens and the earth He hovered over a dark void of nothingness. This is our life apart from Jesus: a dark void of nothingness without purpose, meaning or identity.

Jesus came to be a light for *all* humanity as explained in verse 4. We are illuminated by Him and the void of nothingness filled and formed just like we see in the creation story. I highlight *all* because this isn't just for people who know Jesus; this is a promise for those who don't know Him too.

We live in a world that surrounds us with gloom and doom; with so many people searching for answers these days it's so

important that we hold on to the truth. We need to be fil'
the knowledge of Christ so that we are ready and armed wr ͭ ..
harvest is ripe. People want to be filled with His light and
through us He chooses to make that happen.

As we draw near to Jesus and seek His heart He imparts
wisdom, giving us a yearning desire to see the world become
lighter and more Kingdom filled. He planned it from the beginning,
so let me ask you something else to journal about:

**What would you do if you knew wholeheartedly what Jesus
created you for and that you couldn't fail?**

The world would be a totally different place if we remained
steadfast to the truth. Jesus took time over our creation. He
didn't just throw a load of people out there, we were designed
with great care and attention to detail. He gave us titles, and a
great purpose for His glory. We do have all the skills and
resources within us to do all He's asking of us, so what are we
waiting for?

In verse 5 we see the arrival of a man who knew what his
calling was. He didn't give a hoot what people thought of
him. He's described as very, let's say 'different'. I believe the
attention the writer draws to what he eats, what he wears,
where he spent his time and the way he responds to the people
gives us evidence to suggest his concern is most definitely not
of what people thought of him. What if we were all a little more
like John?

If we weren't so fixated on what people thought of us and
more fixated on what Jesus thinks of us, maybe we wouldn't
hold back so much. If we stepped out in the confidence we
have in Christ we'd achieve much more. We are bound up in
so much fear because that's the way the world has us think.
We see in these next verses repeated that Jesus came into the
world He created, but the world was unaware, which makes

me wonder: If He came now and walked past us in the street, would we know? Would we recognise Him? John did, he was ready.

We are promised in verse 12 that those who embrace Him and take hold of His name are given the authority to become children of God. As a child of God, we have a power within us that is something the world does not have; we carry His very presence within us. John knew this, that's where I believe his confidence came from. He didn't care for people that were ignorant, he knew the truth and he wasn't going to hold back in sharing it. He knew that he wouldn't fail.

In the last section of the study I asked you a question: 'What would you do if you knew wholeheartedly what Jesus created you for and that you couldn't fail?' Let me ask you, what did you write? Was it reams and reams of limitless vision that created a fire in your heart to 'go get 'em' just like John, or did fear hold you back? Was the nagging voice in your head overtaking your vision to see and blocking your creative flow?

John came to teach the truth about Jesus, and he didn't hold back. Verse 15 tells us he announced to the people, 'He's the one! Set your hearts on him!' which is crucial to us knowing why we exist – as we said earlier, apart from Jesus we don't – so my last question for you to ponder is:

How can you set your heart on Jesus and live without fear daily?

If you haven't already it's now time to take the three questions out of this week's study and use them to ponder what God might be saying to you. This is the 'Reflect' part of the study.

Elected Not Elite

WEEK 2

Read John 1:19-34

Last week we looked at our identity in Christ; we learned that apart from Him we are non-existent. Not existing seems a strange concept to our logical minds, doesn't it? But the more we explore our identity in Christ, we begin to see how we could possibly be living a non-existent life.

John had a confidence in what he had been called to do; he seemed to not be fearful of what people thought of him and his focus was on Jesus. This week we are going to explore his nature in a little more detail.

In a world filled with commercialism and materialism it's easy for us to take our eyes off our identity in Christ and begin to look at how we earn our status in society. We covet other people's belongings and long over their positions. We are robbed by comparison and it can become easy to begin to rank ourselves according to the world's score card which inevitably ends up causing doubt and confusion over the truth that sets us free. As I write this, I can already think of areas of my life that cause me confusion and doubt when it comes to who I am in Christ and to who the world defines me as. So, the first question in this week's devotion is:

Can you identify areas of your life that involve confusion or doubt in what the world says versus what God says?

In verse 19 John is interrogated by an entourage of priests and temple servants and we see that if John had not been so bold in what he was called to do, this passive aggressive interrogation could possibly have thrown him off. How often do we get thrown off our course by what the world around us has to say about our lives? I do wonder how I would have responded to their questioning. When it comes to confrontation we go into fight or flight, don't we? Would I have become defensive and responded to their questions with an equal measure of aggression or would I have run away and allowed doubt and confusion to overcome my thought process?

These men wanted to know if John was the prophet that Moses had referred to in Deuteronomy 18:15. Was he anointed and what authority does he hold? John denied that he was either Elijah or the prophet foretold by Moses. They were frantic to know something, anything, about who he was to take back to their leaders. We can see by the text their desperation to go back to those that sent them with knowledge. This makes me wonder how they saw their own identities. They clearly needed to take something back to please the leaders that sent them which gives me reason to believe they needed approval.

Although John approached his calling with courage, and he was bold and confident in the words that he said, he was also humble and meek too. We see that when he denies being a prophet.

However, we read in Matthew 11:11-14 Jesus confirming that there has been none greater than John. Read it for yourself and look at the way Jesus speaks of John with great admiration. We also see that John is in fact the Elijah that was to come. John was not elite, but he had indeed been elected.

Unlike the leaders that sent this entourage of people, he knew that he was elected, set apart, called by God to achieve a task, and that was all that motivated him. He wasn't interested in status, power or authority; he came to make a way for Jesus and that he did. His only motivation was the One who sent him.

I believe that we can use this as a measure for our own lives too. If we think about the things we desire to achieve and measure this against the motivation behind it, we will soon see whether it's 'God led' or 'world led'. Try it as you reflect on today's devotion.

What are the motivations behind the things that you do?

In verse 23 John quotes to the men a prophecy that we can read today in Isaiah 40:3. This prophecy had been given many, many years before John was even born. I imagine that this prophecy was the life mantra for John and his ministry, a rhema word, *meaning a direct word or instruction from God*, that applies to us individually. We carry it in our hearts, stand upon it and it becomes a motivation behind our actions. This word that John quoted back at them was his weapon against the fear that they were trying to inflict upon him. This is a great lesson for us, too, regarding the way in which we look at scripture.

These leaders knew the scriptures back to front but they had no revelation. They had head knowledge but no heart knowledge. They would use the Word of God as a weapon to control others. John, however, did not. He meditated upon those words and allowed God to use them to speak to him and for him. What if we did the same?

Has there been a time God has given you a scripture that relates to your calling or life?

The difference here is the 'ELITE' saw themselves separated from sin; they deemed themselves as set apart and closer to God than anyone else. They used the law to enforce rules and regulations on people and put themselves on a throne of glory.

The 'ELECT' are people hand-picked, chosen by God, bold and courageous, focused on the glory of God yet humble in character. Following His Word and applying that to their lives, literally living and breathing the Word of God day and night.

We, too, are ELECTED by God to work on this earth giving hope where there's dismay, bringing peace to disorder and joy to a world filled with disappointment. We shine in the darkness and radiate the glory of Jesus to all that we meet because we embrace Him, we recognise Him, and we follow Him.

We see some context in The Passion Translation Footnotes, that this all happened in a place which is likely to have been the same place that God parted the water for the children of Israel to cross into the promised land, showing us that this is a new thing God is about to do, leading the people into yet another promised land.

John preached the arrival of Jesus and the very next day he appeared. John recognised Him as soon as he saw Him and announced Him as God's Lamb. As John baptised Jesus we see this image of the dove that was let go when Noah opened the ark. The dove never returned but now the dove comes to its rightful resting place on Jesus, the spirit of peace, the anointing of Jesus our prince of peace. John announces to those that were present in verse 34 that he can tell us for sure that Jesus is the son of God.

John was elected to make way for Jesus' arrival. There were lots of practical things attached to that job, there were many things that John would have had to do and experience before the verses we've read today. Can you think of what those might have been?

We've discovered that we, too, are elected by God, by divine appointment, set apart and chosen for a purpose. You may not know what that is yet or you may have had revelation to what that might be. Maybe you are doing what you've been called to do but know that there's more. Wherever you are in that process, spend some time reflecting on what God wants to say to you about your purpose on this earth and the questions given.

What Do You Want?

WEEK 3

Read John 1:35-51

So far, we've looked at our identity in Christ and how that can become blurred if we start to look to the world to define us. Last week we learnt about John and how he was elected by God to make way for the arrival of Jesus and the beginning of His ministry, much to the despair of the religious leaders who questioned John. We saw that those leaders had an image of themselves as being set apart from sin and closer to God than any other; they gave themselves an elite status.

We explored the differences between the elect and the elite and came to the conclusion that only the Word of God can define us. The questions I set were surrounding calling and purpose and for us to dig a little bit deeper into that with the help of the Holy Spirit.

This week we are going to look at what happened when Jesus called His first disciples. Again, a group of people elected by Him to support Him in His work on earth.

By all accounts 'What do you want?' are the first words spoken by Jesus in the account of the Gospels. In verse 38, two of John's disciples left him and began to follow Jesus. Jesus turns on His foot and looks at these men, 'What do you want?' He says. Can you imagine it?

As I read this portion of scripture I started to think about the garden of Eden. Adam and Eve were filled with shame for disobeying God as they ran and hid from Him. The question asked here was 'Where are you?' Here in the perfect garden we see our creator pursuing humanity but in this portion we see humanity pursuing God as the disciples respond with, 'Rabbi, where are you staying?'

This one question is very thought provoking: what is it I want in following Jesus?

The first time I encountered the love of Jesus and knew for sure He was real was a time in my life where I'd come to the end of myself. I was in a place that was dark, I was drinking a lot, my marriage was in a mess and I didn't know who I was. I had been invited by a business associate to attend a church she went to so I thought, what's the harm in that? I think if I'm honest I admired that lady and I coveted what she had. I wanted her confidence, charisma and business sense so that's the main reason I went along. I thought, 'If it's good enough for her then it's good enough for me.'

We walked into lots of smiles and hugs, which was a bit weird; coming from a family that's not all that touchy-feely, I was already way out of my comfort zone! Then the worship began and these people were singing at the top of their voices. The music was loud and very modern, not like the wooden pews, hymns and Bible readings I had expected. We came to the end of the second song and people were making funny noises, their hands lifted up. All of a sudden a man from behind me began to bellow out in some strange language and a lady to the side of him was singing angelic sounds but no words. Everything within me wanted to run but I somehow knew that I was in the right place. I wanted to know more. This experience reminds me of that moment in verse 42 when Andrew brought Simon to meet Jesus and it's described as Jesus 'gazed' upon Simon. I believe that in that moment Jesus looked into Peter's spirit and they connected far beyond natural comprehension. This is what happened in my heart the day I entered the doors of that church. Just as the disciples asked, 'Where do you abide?' I, too, wanted to know what this was all about, who was it they were singing to? How could they do all these strange things so freely with no care and complete abandon?

Can you remember what it was you wanted when you first met Jesus?

Verses 43-51 introduce us to Nathanael, a man who I can relate to at this time in my life. Nathanael was a doubter. His comment 'What good thing comes from Nazareth?' was very sarcastic, I think, and makes me wonder what lies behind his comment.

The day that we first decided to attend church there had been a group of ladies discussing this big women's conference in Leeds. It was £65 per ticket and it was over three days which would have meant two nights in a hotel too. I certainly couldn't afford this at the time and I was far too distracted with what I'd just seen to even contemplate anything more. We left and I spent the next few days in a hazy wonder at what I'd witnessed and felt. Over the course of about three days I spent lots of time reflecting and wondering if what I felt and saw was real, and there were many occurrences of me gazing up at the sky asking God to present Himself to me, whilst awaiting a miraculous bolt of lightning and a loud deep voice calling my name!

The following Monday morning I was preparing to leave home for a training event I was running when I received a text from one of the ladies from the church, who had met me once. She offered to cover the cost of the ticket to the women's conference and I could pay her back when I was in a better position. She said in her text that God had told her to. It completely baffled me. Firstly, I'd been asking God to present Himself to me for days and He hadn't said a word to me so why did He speak to her and not me?! Secondly, why on earth would she pay for a ticket for a complete stranger? I'm still waiting for the £50 back from a friend of five years or more so what made her think I'm trustworthy? All this thinking made me extremely late for the event I was going to so, in a rush, I got on my way still trying to process what had just happened. The next thing I knew my car was side on, having left a busy dual carriageway at a ridiculous speed stopping just 500 yards from the end of a bridge.

You guessed it – I crashed my car. At that point I got the miraculous entry from God. There were a number of things that should have happened but didn't. Firstly, I was driving at a really irresponsible speed as I lost control of the car and hit the left-hand barrier. The metal from the barrier pulled out most of the underneath of my car and the car should have actually been overturned by the impact. The fact that the car stopped right at the point it did was also a bit of a mystery. I wasn't wearing a seatbelt but I didn't move an inch from my seat despite the impact. The next thing that happened was the arrival of the emergency services which I knew I'd be in trouble for. It was clear to the police officer that I had been driving irresponsibly but he decided that he wouldn't proceed with the paperwork to investigate further because there wasn't anyone else involved. The roads were wet and the sun low and he was satisfied that I could have hit oil on the road and lost control of the car. He was also amazed at the fact I was uninjured and my car remained upright. The final blessing was that the client I was serving for the training event was late setting off and only five minutes behind me on the same stretch of road. She picked me up and took me to the event I needed to be at while my poor car was taken off to car heaven.

All those blessings in one very short but long morning and I still found myself wondering where God was in it all.

The purpose of me sharing this story with you is during that whole journey I was distracted, looking for reasons to doubt even when God showed up valiantly saving me from death. I still analysed the whole situation. I was like Nathanael: what good thing could come from following Jesus? I was so distracted with doubt that I totally missed the answers to my prayers.

Could it be possible that you are missing a blessing by being overcome by doubt?

The following week sealed the deal for me. I returned to church battered and bruised, not physically but mentally. I'd spent the whole week trying to figure it all out. I'd become so depressed that I questioned why I didn't die in that car. My husband and I were further apart than ever, and I'd drunk so much the night before that my head was fuzzy. On the journey to church the car was filled with an atmosphere of hatred as we screamed and shouted at one another in front of our young boys. We arrived at the car park and neither of us wanted to enter the building. I know that the Holy Spirit gave us the courage to get out of the car. The service had already begun and the music was playing as we entered the main hall. As I walked towards our seats my heart was overcome. The words to the song cutting into my soul like nothing I've experienced before: 'Take me deeper than my feet could ever wander.' The tears began to flow, which again was a miracle as I never cried in public. No one would ever see my emotions because I was conditioned to hide them. I sobbed that morning from a place within me that I never knew existed. The pastor and women's leader came over and prayed over me. As they prayed I cried harder. I cried so much that I thought I was going to be sick. I began to make a noise I'd never made in my life; it was a noise filled with authority and power and it came from somewhere in my body I couldn't explain. It was loud but relieving at the same time. By the time I stopped I felt lighter and different in some way. It was difficult to explain but all the heaviness and oppression I walked into church with that morning had gone. The Holy Spirit filled me to overflowing that day; there wasn't any room for darkness because the light that filled me extinguished all darkness. In that moment I knew how to answer Jesus' question: 'What do you want?'

My answer: 'To be filled to overflowing with this life-giving light all my days!'

That experience is the moment of pivotal change for me on this journey. I believe that I was so desperate for Jesus in that moment, so done with myself, that I had no alternative but to surrender to Him. From that moment on, my life has changed and continues to change, but in answering that question I now know what I want in Him is what He wants for me.

What pivotal moments on your journey could help you to answer Jesus' question?

Say Cheers for Endless Joy!

WEEK 4

Read John 2:1-11

Life is busy, isn't it? I have three children aged 2, 7 and 8. I'm a business owner, I do lots of voluntary work and I run a weekly Bible study at church, so I can end up feeling a little worn out if I'm not careful. Fridays for me are a day to get the chores done. I clean the house from top to bottom, I do the food shop and I take care of the washing so that we have uniforms ready for Monday. I do this so that I know by 7pm when the kids are in bed on Friday evening, I can pour a nice glass of wine, sit back and relax, and this brings me great joy.

Here in chapter 2 we see Jesus, His mother and disciples at a wedding in a place called Cana. The footnotes of The Passion Translation tell us that the word 'Cana' means 'land of reeds', which points to the fragile nature of humanity. And we are *very* fragile, aren't we?

One of my favourite things to do is to people watch. I find myself mesmerised at the people around me when I'm at the school gates or in a coffee shop in town watching the world go by. What strikes me is the busyness of the world. I often find myself thinking about the burdens that people are carrying as they rush along in the day to day of ordinary life and wonder, 'What if they stopped to process what Jesus did for us and what that means to the quality of life we are living.' What if we took our issues to Jesus and allowed Him, the Father and the Holy Spirit to help us with those deep-rooted lies, would that help us to slow down a little? Jesus said that He came to give us life in abundance. What if we trusted Him enough to allow Him to do that? I believe that this abundant life is one filled with joy that doesn't just last a while, one that is endless and limitless. Since meeting Him for the first time I've been determined to pursue that life He has promised me. Let me ask you a question to ponder:

What do you feel would enable you to have more joy in your day-to-day life right now?

This wedding took place on Tuesday, and there was a reason for this. The Hebrew week started on a Sunday, so this wedding was on the third day of the week. The third day in our Christian faith is very significant to us but back then Jesus hadn't yet been revealed in glory.

Even before this took place the third day was significant. The reason being that in the story of Creation, on the third day God blessed it twice (see Genesis 1:10-12). Twice God said 'and it is good' and so this particular day was considered by the people to be doubly blessed and that is why most wedding ceremonies would be held on a Tuesday.

So, let's picture this doubly blessed wedding day: the party is in full swing, everyone is enjoying themselves, the speeches are done, and the drinks are flowing, there's laughter and joy throughout, then disaster strikes! There's no more wine.

Envisage being the wedding planner at this do? It would be a total party stopper, wouldn't it?

Can you imagine being a guest at the wedding? Or even worse, the bride and groom? Just feel the disappointment for a moment, the master of ceremonies approaches and whispers the news in your ear, how would you feel? Thankfully it didn't come to that!

The significance of the story begins to come to us as we dig deeper into the context of the scriptures.

The place where the wedding is held points to our fragility as human beings.

The wine running out points to the joy that we place upon things.

How often do we hear the phrase, 'I'll be happy when . . .'? I'll be happy when Friday comes, I'll be happy when winter is over, I'll be happy when we get a bigger house, I'll be happy when I get a new job . . . it goes on and on.

Happiness is not joy: happiness depends on circumstances; joy is a state of mind. We humans love to depend on circumstances to dictate which we choose. The problem with this is, things are temporary and the feeling that they give us is limited to a time frame; by doing so we set the bar so high we become reliant on things to make us happy, and this feeling doesn't last, it runs out, just like the wine.

By engaging in this consumer lifestyle, we have to strive. Working harder to get the promotion or the money to buy the things that make us happy. Thus, adding pressure to our lives and over time we become worn out. When we don't recognise how tired we are becoming and continue to strive it results in burnout. This is why we see so many issues with mental health in the world today. We fill our hands so much that there's no time to just 'be'. We are called human beings, not human doings, we weren't created to strive this much. Our human existence may be more joyful if we would focus more on being in the moment rather than doing 'stuff' to fill the moment.

I want you to think about something in the 'Reflect' section of today's devotional:

What are you striving for? How is that serving you? How joyful do you feel right now?

Looking at verse 2 we can see that Mary knew the anointing of her son. She informs Him that the wine had run dry and His response was to ask why He should be concerned with this, His time had not yet come. I don't know the reason for this, I'm not a theologian, but I do know that He did not mean He didn't care. The signs and wonders we see throughout this wonderful book point to the reason Jesus came and here He's creating a wonderful picture of how He gives us endless and limitless joy. Mary knew this and instructed the servants to do as He tells them.

I wonder, what if we did as He told us?

There have been so many instances in my life I've been disobedient. How different would it have been if only I'd have listened?

But Jesus never wastes anything. Those times things haven't gone the right way for me because of my disobedience I've learned from. Those lessons have formed and shaped my future. I've developed in my relationship with Him and become more attuned to the sound of His voice; after all, it's said, 'He brings all things together for our good' (Romans 8:28).

Jesus tells the servants to use the six stone pots nearby and fill them with water. These pots are another significant sign. The pots were used to perform ceremonial cleansing prior to prayer, a *religious ritual* of the day. There was a *duty* where the people would need to be cleansed before entering the presence of God. According to The Passion Translation, six is the number for man, as God created man on the sixth day. The water *could* represent religion, meaningless, tasteless and transparent. The wine is the joy that's run out.

Jesus takes something that is *religious*, *ritualistic* and done out of *duty* and uses it to provide something sweet tasting, aromatic and joyful. He didn't just create one bottle either. It is said that out of those pots He created between 120 and 150 gallons of wine – in other words, an endless supply.

The thing with religion, rituals and doing things out of duty is that we are bound to them. It's rigid and to be honest not very fulfilling. The motivation behind the action is that I have to do it, not that I want to do it. When we have to do something, we don't necessarily do it joyfully, we do it as a tick-box exercise.

What could be something you do rigidly at the moment?

You are a Temple of God

WEEK 5

Read John 2:12-25

Last week we learnt that if we allow Him, Jesus will provide our lives with limitless joy. We recognised that a measure of joy in the world today is outward circumstances and possessions. We also discovered that we are fragile beings and that sometimes things can come along that destroy our ability to worship God in the way we were created to.

This next part of the book of John pictures a scene of greed and how that implicated the relationship between people who wanted to worship God. A people that longed to give of themselves in worship to their creator were being taken advantage of and this was not a joyful sight to Jesus.

The picture that emerges here is a temple filled with gluttony, many selling oxen, lambs and doves – and they weren't cheap! No, it says they were sold for exorbitant prices.

It was drawing near to Passover and there were Gentiles approaching to worship at the temple. These greedy salesmen knew that the Gentiles would want to bring a sacrifice to God, and they were cashing in! Not only were they charging over the odds for their produce but they also cashed in on the exchange rate. The currency the Gentiles had wasn't one accepted in this part of the country, so they needed to exchange it and they didn't get a good rate either. The people who arrived at the temple that day just wanted to worship the Father, but the barriers placed in their way were sickening to the heart of Jesus.

We read through the portion of scripture and are struck by Jesus turning over the tables and creating a whip out of rope. He seems extremely angry. But this anger isn't one of violent outburst: the tables were turned so that nothing else could be placed on them; the whip was made to move out the animals. It's not an image of Him using these articles to inflict pain and suffering on those in the wrong here. It's not in His nature, but I can see why this scene could cause confusion to people. His only motive was to clear this temple to allow in those who wanted to worship His Father.

Jesus feels the same about the barriers in our life that affect our worship. With so many distractions around us today I believe that He could get as passionate about our situation as He did back then. Why don't you ponder this next question and see if there's anything holding you back that He can remove for you.

Are there barriers that get in the way of your worship?

Once Jesus has turned the tables and begins to empty the temple, His authority is challenged. Who was He to say that this shouldn't go on? What right did He have to say who should worship there and who shouldn't? His response was, 'After you've destroyed this temple, I will raise it up again in three days' (John 2:19). They were astounded to hear such a thing and mocked His response; it had taken them 46 years to build that structure and here He was telling them that He would raise it again in three days!

We know that Jesus was speaking of Himself here: He was the temple that they would destroy. He was speaking about the resurrection which would be the supreme sign of His authority. Effectively the resurrection would make the temple obsolete; there would be no need for a holy place because He would return and enter our hearts. The church would be a body of people, each one of us individually making up parts of His body on earth, continuing to do His work (see 1 Corinthians 3:16 and 6:19).

If you are reading from The Passion Translation here and have access to the footnotes, you'll also see this interesting fact. Our bodies, which are now carriers of the same Holy Spirit that raised Jesus from the grave and therefore a temple, have 23 pairs of chromosomes which makes a total of 46, the same number of years it took to build the temple. How crazy is that?

The attention to detail that went into the creation of the human body never ceases to amaze me. The care to create each and every one just so is unfathomable. What's more astounding is that He chose to make our bodies His home. Each one of us a living, breathing, walking, talking vessel for the creator of the heavens and the earth. That kind of blows those barriers we just talked about out of the water, doesn't it? I cannot help but worship God at the thought of all this. If I fixed my mind on this at the beginning of each day and continually kept that in my mind throughout the day how different would my life look? Take some time to think about it for yourself, grab your journal and a pen and answer this question:

How does it make you feel to know you are a temple of God?

As we reach the end of chapter 2, in verses 23-25 we see that the number of people who followed Jesus began to grow because of the miracles they were seeing Him perform and it's no wonder, is it? People were beginning to see the freedom He was here to bring. Healing and suffering were being diminished before their eyes and they wanted in. He was removing the restrictions that had been placed upon them by legalism and religion and showing them that they were free to learn to love the Lord their God just as He loves them.

However, verse 23 states that their following Him was because of the miraculous signs they had seen. It was because of what they had seen, not what they believed, and Jesus knew this. The text says that Jesus did not yet entrust Himself to them, because He knew how fickle human hearts can be. He didn't need anyone to tell Him about human nature, *for He fully understood what man was capable of doing*.

And we are fickle, aren't we? I am. From one day to the next I can change my mind; my husband can never keep up! On a serious note, though, our motives can sometimes be wrong and Jesus knows that. In order to keep our hearts right we need to regularly check in on our motive. As we carry the spirit of Jesus within us we have responsibility to glorify Him but, for reasons we've already discussed, we can end up being overwhelmed by the circumstances around us. We are told in Romans 12 to continually renew our minds and this is why.

We must make sure that the decisions we make are led of the Holy Spirit and not based on the world around us. By regularly assessing our time and how we spend it, along with the motive behind that, we can begin to see where that desire comes from. Then according to where the desire comes from, we can decide what to do with it. I do this regularly, and I find things that I don't believe were planted by God. I give them back to Him and ask that His will be done. I then generally find that doors will open and close accordingly.

Try it for yourself in your journal now, the last question for this week's Reflect is:

What is the motive behind some of the desires you have and spend time on?

Endless Life

WEEK 6

Read John 3:1-21

In chapter 3 we are introduced to one of the Jewish leaders, Nicodemus. He's described in The Passion Translation as a prominent religious leader so we know that he must have been quite well known. It also describes that he is a member of the Jewish ruling council. Nicodemus means 'conqueror', which leads me to think wandering around discreetly wouldn't be something he did often. I'd have thought with his clout he could wander boldly wherever he liked, but on this particular evening, in the dark, we see him visit Jesus discreetly. Undercover, a covert operation so as not to be noticed by anyone else. Why was that? Was it the fear of what other people would think?

It leads me to think about my own relationship with Jesus and whether or not, at times, I might hide my faith in Him in order to fit in. One of the biggest root issues I deal with in my life is fear of rejection. I've always had a fear of not fitting in. In fact, in my teenage years I made some pretty stupid choices in order to fit in. My point being here, I know that this fear exists, and I know that potentially I can make decisions on the basis of me fitting in with a group of people. Being aware of this issue helps me to process the decisions I make. I have to be continually checking on myself, just as I said in last week's devotion. I have to analyse my thoughts before I make my opinion known.

Do I agree because I want people to like me or do I disagree because I know that it conflicts my faith?

To live with integrity is something that Jesus wants for us all. Each of us playing a part of His body means that we can be there for one another and assist in these moments of fear. I know that I have fellow believers around me that I can ask to hold me accountable for my actions and that comforts me. To be a person of integrity means to always do the right thing even when others aren't watching. What Nicodemus did here was the right thing but hidden because he feared what others would think.

Are there times you may have hidden your faith in order to fit in?

Jesus and Nicodemus go on to have a conversation about how a person can perceive the Kingdom of God. They must experience rebirth in order to do so. Nicodemus could not comprehend that statement and the image he speaks of is quite amusing. His logical human mind could not comprehend how a human being with grey hair might go back into his mother's womb and be born again! That's so human, isn't it? We are so logical, it's no wonder we totally miss the wonder of God in some circumstances.

Jesus explains that we need to be born from above, of water and Spirit-wind (John 3:5). Looking deeper into the footnotes, The Passion Translation describes it as this: 'The water is the cleansing of the Word, the Word is Jesus' (see 1 Peter 1:23). Jesus goes on to explain that only natural things can be born in a natural world. If we want to see the power and authority of God then we must humble ourselves and be reborn by the supernatural realm. It's certainly a humbling experience, wouldn't you agree? We must shift our human, logical thinking, our own perspective, surrender and agree to be reborn.

Jesus goes on to say, 'For the Spirit-wind blows as it chooses. You can hear its sound, but you don't know where it came from or where it's going. So it is within the hearts of those who are Spirit-born!' (John 3:8).

To be honest, it's no wonder Nicodemus didn't understand! It must have sounded so mysterious and it still is – living a life led by the Holy Spirit is utterly mysterious.

I must say that my life has been so much more exciting since I've surrendered it to Jesus. The adventures we go on together are amazing. There have been times on my walk I've encountered visions or ideas that to the human mind are ridiculous but I know that they are Holy Spirit given.

The word for 'blow' in verse 8 can also be translated as 'breathe' and the word 'sound' can be translated 'voice'. The whisper of the Holy Spirit breathes life into our spiritually dry bones, the voice we hear deep within our heart urging us to 'Go!' is the One calling us to live for more. It's just so exciting!

Here's another question to mull over at the end of today's devotional:

What visions, ideas or creations has the Holy Spirit whispered into your heart?

Being led by the Holy Spirit is living life to the fullness as far as I'm concerned. I love it!

John 3:16 is likely to be the most quoted scripture in the world to date. I'm taking a wild guess here as I don't know for a fact that's true. But in my opinion, Christian or not, I think that most people can quote that verse without reading it from the Bible. The thing with recitals is that they can become repetitive and mundane. We repeat the words and the more we do they lose their meaning. The power of John 3:16 is lost the more it is repeated. We take it for granted.

As I began to study this verse for a Bible study I was leading, I began to realise just how powerful and life changing it is when understood in its entirety.

When we read the verse, we see that the word 'perish' comes before 'everlasting life'. I'm looking at The Passion Translation here but in any translation the word 'perish' comes first. I find that odd; for something to perish it must cease to be alive. The fact that it's placed before everlasting life here, I wonder, are we to be encouraged to think about the contrast of perishing and everlasting life?

I believe that the reason the word 'perish' is placed before the promise of everlasting life is because it is possible to be living and breathing but perish at the same time. In one of our earlier devotions we discovered that apart from Jesus we cease to exist. This is the same. Without the Holy Spirit leading we fail to receive the everlasting life Jesus died to give us. I don't believe that this everlasting life is just one of eternity, I believe that it begins now. Jesus tells us later in the book of John that He came so that we could have life in its fullness. Could that mean the everlasting life that we are missing now. Could it be that we are perishing now?

Pondering all of this gives me reason to asses my own life: is it one that's full to overflowing or do I feel like I'm curling up, waiting for the end of my earthly walk and wondering what heaven will be like?

I don't believe that being a Christian just means that we have hope in eternity, we can begin that life now, we can serve Jesus as we navigate the world. We can be led of the Holy Spirit every minute of every day if we choose to be. I think that an everlasting life is one that's vibrant, joyful and exciting. I don't think that it's one which is mundane and unsatisfying. What do you think?

What does everlasting life mean to you? Are you perishing in any area of your life?

Humble Progression

WEEK 7

Read John 3:22-36

When I read the first verse of this next portion, I imagine the scenery of the beautiful countryside and find my mind wander towards how amazing it would have been to be baptised by Jesus and His disciples! I love baptism time at church. The testimonies, the joy as people burst through the water, it's just wonderful. Every time I find myself wanting to do it all over again. I loved how close I felt to Jesus when I decided to proclaim my faith and be born again of water. I left my old life at the bottom of that pool and found a new life waiting for me as I burst through the rim!

We go from this serene and peaceful image to one of dispute. The text doesn't tell us who the Jewish man was that they were arguing with but it certainly shifted the atmosphere. There was disruption and as a result of this disagreement we begin to see rivalry. John's disciples didn't seem to be happy about others baptising larger crowds.

It makes me think of the world today. We see a lot of rivalry, don't we? Things can be nicely ticking along then suddenly we stumble across disgruntlement. The dispute can involve us directly or not but either way it can be unsettling. When we find ourselves caught in this experience it helps to remember that this is not from Jesus, we do not fight against flesh and blood. No matter what the circumstance we need to fix our eyes on Him.

Jesus calls us to unity. Ephesians 4:1-6 in *The Message* says it like this:

In light of all this, here's what I want you to do. While I'm locked up here, a prisoner for the Master, I want you to get out there and walk – better yet, run! – on the road God called you to travel. I don't want any of you sitting around on your hands. I don't want anyone strolling off, down some path that goes nowhere. And mark that you do this with humility and discipline – not in fits and starts, but steadily, pouring yourselves out for each other in acts of love, alert at noticing differences and quick at mending fences.

You were all called to travel on the same road and in the same direction, so stay together, both outwardly and inwardly. You have one Master, one faith, one baptism, one God and Father of all, who rules over all, works through all, and is present in all. Everything you are and think and do is permeated with Oneness.

How beautiful is that? We are called together on the same road, with the same goal in mind, no matter what we are, to be quick at mending fences. Get over whatever it is we are holding on to. Rivalry is not something that achieves the unity expressed in this passage. So, without further ado, let's do some journaling around our first question of the week:

Can you identify any rivalry in your life now?

I really do love John; his explanation is that Jesus came to claim His bride, He is the bridegroom. So why do we insist on these claims over property or people as we see in this passage?

Pride. Pride is the root cause of this problem. The opposite to pride is humility and that's what we see so beautifully described in Ephesians 4. For us to reduce our pride we must think of ourselves less and less. John describes it like this: it's necessary for Him to increase and for me to be diminished (see John 3:30).

I have three children and I often use the term, 'Well done, I'm so proud of you.' This isn't the pride that I'm talking about here. The pride I'm talking about is one that says, 'I deserve this.' It's thinking that we are owed something based on our performance. It's having the opinion that we are more knowledgeable and better than others. When we think in this way, we find that we place ourselves higher than others around us. As people begin to notice our posture, we find opposition and we encourage rivalry. Then, we work harder at becoming better, we focus on the wrong goal. Just like the people building the tower in Babel, we are trying to make a name for ourselves. With this in mind the next question to reflect on this week is:

Are there any areas in your life you are trying to make a name for yourself?

The problem with making a name for ourselves is that we end up trying to earn the respect of people. Our eyes end up being fixed on the wrong god. Whether that's a boss, a leader, a career, a business, that thing becomes an idol. Our gaze transfixes on what we can do in order to make it to the next step. Our lives become a sequence of goals that earn us a materialistic prize at the end of it. But we know that's not what Jesus wants for us. We learnt in one of the previous devotions that our joy is not defined by things in this world. If we determine our success on those things it won't be long before it runs dry, like the wine at the wedding in Cana. It's simply not sustainable. John says it like this:

For the one who is from the earth belongs to the earth and speaks from the natural realm. But the One who comes from above is above everything and speaks of the highest realm of all! His message is about what he has seen and experienced, even though people don't accept it. Yet those who embrace his message know in their hearts that it's the truth. (John 3:31-33)

This chapter is about humility. It's about choosing to allow Jesus sovereignty over our lives, to submit to Him as the bridegroom of the church. What we see in the chapter is a pride-filled debate that is centred on vanity and rivalry. These types of disgruntlements continually cause division in the world today. It's one of the devil's favourite tools: if he can divide unity, he can destroy the body of Christ. We cannot allow this to happen.

In the last part of this chapter John goes on to explain that God has poured out the fullness of the Holy Spirit upon Jesus without limitation. We are to trust in Him. If we don't trust in Him, we will not see life in its fullness. If we continue to lean on our understanding, we will continue to be disappointed. We must allow Jesus to be seen more and more, to do so is to submit all things into His hands.

What will you lay back into His hands today?

Leaving the Past Behind

WEEK 8

Read John 4:1-30

This week we read about a lady who has been terribly mistreated. I can't begin to think about some of the things that she had endured during her short lifetime. We can see as we read some indicators of the shame that she felt.

I imagine this lady opening her eyes to another day of loneliness. As she arises, her thoughts immediately filled with embarrassment and shame. The text explains the time of day that she chose to go to collect water; it's a time in which she wouldn't see anyone around, so with this in mind we know that she was avoiding any confrontation. When I think of her posture as she walks along, I see a picture of her shoulders low and her head bowed down, her gaze transfixed on the floor in fear of seeing any other person. Maybe she was pondering life. I feel her sadness as I imagine her mulling over the marriages she's had and abandonment she's endured. I think we can all empathise with this lady and I can certainly relate to this story. The day I met with Jesus for the first time I was filled with regret, shame, guilt and sadness for my life and all I'd done leading up to then. I was bound to a cycle of continually getting it wrong. My children and husband had no hope in me, I was sure of it. I was a no-one that had done some terrible things and made some awful life decisions and I was living my life in constant fear that those choices would one day catch up with me.

How can you relate to the woman at the well?

Pre-Jesus I was a drinker and a 'recreational' drug user, to the point that I would depend on these things to go out into a social environment. I liked who I was when I was high and drunk because people didn't see the real me. They saw a fun loving, more confident version of me. I use the word 'recreational' lightly, because the more I used, the more I relied upon these things to get me through each day. People didn't see the pain and shame I was covering up. I found that men liked me too. This was a big thing for me because I was desperate to be loved. These one-night experiences filled that gap for a short time, and I felt loved, although it was false. I would go out night after night flirtatiously gaining approval from anyone who would give me attention. Unbeknown to me at the time I was making these choices and using the vices to plaster over many years of feeling abandoned. It was self-abuse. It worked for a short time but then, I'd go home and wake the next morning to feel the pain of rejection once again. This would be with the added pain of the abuse I'd put my body through, and the shame would grow; there in the mirror would be a reflection of someone I completely despised, and the cycle would continue. If I was lucky enough to have drugs left from the night before or money in the bank I would go and do it all again, if not I'd sleep the day away ignoring calls from my family and friends, wrapped up in the pain of the shame.

Back to the road where the lady is walking along with only her bucket for company. Imagine her scurrying to get the job done quickly, thus reducing the risk of being seen, when suddenly she hears a voice, 'Give me a drink of water.' With a jolt she looks up and behold, there perched on the source she would collect her water from is the source of the living water that would change her life forever! What a shock! I think her spirit would have stirred from the moment He spoke. Not only that, I'd imagine her adrenaline would have kicked into defence mode – this was a Jewish man asking a Samaritan for a drink!

I love that Jesus asked this lady for something that she needed from Him. When God is pursuing me to change something, I generally find that it begins with a question. Here we see Jesus asking her to quench His thirst, but beneath His question is a motive. A motive to quench her thirst for freedom. He proved that His motive was freedom in speaking to her in the first place, a Jew asking a Samaritan for something life giving. He didn't label her as the world did and He went on to explain to her that He knew the circumstances of her life. His motive to give her a new identity, just as He did to me. The day I met Jesus there was a question: did I want to wash myself of all the guilt I carried? In answering this question, I began to work with Him to understand why I'd made those decisions. I began to understand that He forgave me, and I was able to forgive others. At that moment I began to feel freedom and fulfilment for the first time in my life. I was loved. Undeniably. Unconditionally. Each label I'd attached to myself over the years removed. Adopted into a family that loved unconditionally, a child of God. The unconditional love I'd spent my life to date seeking, that same love the woman at the well longed for, met us both where we were and gave us a new identity.

What about you? Ponder this as you journal in the 'Reflect' section of this week's devotion.

Who does Jesus say you are?

The moment of freedom I've spoken of here didn't happen the day I surrendered my life to Jesus. It happened over a period of time and still now I'm discovering more and more. The day I got my new identity was my first time visiting a women's conference. From the minute I entered the arena the presence of God was immense. I went back in time that day, I was 8-year-old me again and my Father scooped me up on to His lap and as He stroked my hair and held me tight, He whispered a number of truths over my heart. He explained all that I'd done up to that moment, I saw areas of my life where He'd been calling me. I returned from that conference to never be the same again. Just like the woman at the well I was amazed that He knew everything I'd ever done, and He loved me.

The woman's response to His knowledge was a barrage of questions. I, too, had many questions, and still do; it's why we continue to grow. I love that the text states she was confused (John 4:25). As we read on, though, despite her confusion she moved. She went back to her village and told everyone about Jesus. She chucked the bucket and ran to the people she began the day avoiding. She still had questions, yet she went and changed her name; she was no longer the woman who had been married five times and was living in sin with a sixth; she was the first evangelist of the Bible! I think that sometimes we spend far too long trying to get all the answers before we move. Had I stayed in the same inquisitive mindset after the conference I attended I wouldn't be writing this devotional now. There are many things that still confuse me, but God is not the author of confusion (1 Corinthians 14:33) and we don't need to have it all figured out to step into our purpose. This lady stepped straight into hers and became the first female evangelist and bought a whole village of people to Jesus. She was chosen, she was called, she was elected by the creator of the heavens and the earth. The people who once despised her ran to Jesus because of her testimony.

Now that's powerful!

What purpose could Jesus be asking you to step into?

Are You Ready?

WEEK 9

Read John 4:31-42

Last week we read all about the transformation of the life of the woman at the well. We see that by the encounter she had with Jesus she went on to play a part in the transformation of the people in the village in which she lived. These people would have been the ones that pitied her, but they all found salvation through her. As the village people emerge towards Jesus and His disciples, He takes the opportunity to teach the disciples about the harvest. When we see lives changed through Jesus Christ there will be a harvest to gather. Since my life has been so impacted by Him and His love has moulded and shaped me into the newfound identity I have, I too have managed to bring some people around me to find that love for themselves. That's what we are called to do. I'd like to begin this devotion reflecting on how you, too, can show people the love of Jesus.

Can you name three people in your life now that you can pray for to come to know the love of Jesus?

When the disciples return, they begin to mother Jesus about eating. I can imagine it now, 'Come on, Teacher, You've not eaten, You need to keep up Your strength!' Jesus tells them His feast has been given to Him by doing the will of His Father.

I tend to feel like this when I've finished teaching a Bible study or finished writing one of these devotionals; it's something that fills me with so much satisfaction.

Each month there's a praise and worship night we host in our church. It's a free-flowing evening with no agenda other than to follow the Holy Spirit. I always leave them feeling full to overflowing. One that stands out to me most was on Easter Sunday. We used the time to praise like children and we really lifted the roof that night. We had so many people getting up to give testimony of the amazing things that Jesus had done in their lives. I literally felt I could burst when we came away. It's a satisfaction that I can't describe but I think that this is what Jesus is describing when He tells His disciples of the feast He's received.

His fullness comes from our freedom and when we are restored to our rightful relationship with the Father, He is complete. We each become a part of His body on earth, giving of ourselves to Him and for Him, in turn receiving that same fullness.

What is it that gives you this fullness?

Once He's told them of His feast, Jesus goes on to explain to His disciples that the harvest is ready. The people are coming, and their hearts are like vast fields of ripened grain ready for a spiritual harvest.

One of my friends never misses an opportunity to invite people to church. Whenever there's an event she thinks will help people understand who Jesus is, she asks those on her heart to come along. One time she invited someone to a big worship event, the lady came along and seemed to enjoy herself. When my friend followed up with this lady after the event her response was that she'd enjoyed it and thought my friend was amazing at leading worship, but religion wasn't her thing. She said that her motive to come was to just listen to my friend sing. This was disappointing but my friend didn't miss the opportunity to explain to this lady that her gift, her singing, was from God and that it didn't belong to her. There was a seed sewn that day and some food for thought for this lady. The harvest wasn't ready, but my friend did not miss the opportunity to bring it back to the creator.

A few months later, this lady got in touch with my friend to say her mother was in hospital really unwell. She was very upset and had no idea what to do as she sat at her mother's bedside watching her struggle to breathe. Without a second thought my friend knew what she needed to do: she stepped out in courage and instructed this lady to lay hands on her mother's chest. She then recorded herself praying and sent it to the lady for her to play over her mother. As the lady did as instructed her mother's breathing became less laboured and by the time the prayer had finished her mother was sat upright in bed! That was another seed sown.

This lady didn't come to Jesus following this event but it's still another shoot off the initial seed that had been planted by my friend inviting her to church. Had she given up on sharing her faith this miracle wouldn't have happened.

We don't know what God will go on to do in her life but that's the glory of playing a part of His body: we each work on different areas.

Another example of sowing and harvesting I can give are the people that decided to pray for me at 8 years old. These people were parents of a girl I went to school with. My mum had fallen upon hard times and they invited us to church; we went along, and my mum decided it wasn't for her, so we never went back. Twenty odd years later this couple walked into the church I was attending. I'd been a Christian about two months at this point and they were very surprised to see me there! As we chatted through my testimony the lady pulled her Bible from her bag and opened it up to a page that had a folded note inside it.

The note was written by me to her daughter. She had found it one day as she cleared her daughter's room and from that day to this, the lady had prayed for me to come to know the love of Jesus. She had no idea where in the world I was but continued to pray. All those years later, there I was, stood in front of her knowing full well the love of Jesus. Not only was her seed planted but it had taken root and God honoured her to see the harvest before her eyes. She prayed for me but stood before her now was not only me but my husband and my three boys, all serving as our parts to Christ's body.

Whether we plant the seed or not, God will always reap His harvest in His time. It's just up to us whether we play a part in His plan. We can be alert and attuned to His instruction or we can go through our lives with our eyes fixed on something else, the choice is ours. There is nothing more satisfying than seeing someone surrender their lives to Jesus and identifying who they are in Him. He allows us to play that part and, in this scripture, He's giving the disciples a village of people to harvest. If we listen and obey, He will give that village to us, too.

That day many became believers; not only that but they begged Jesus to stay longer and teach them. We need to long for His presence without agenda just like these people did. Someone that meets Jesus and hungers for the Word of God is a fruitful harvest. It's the truth that will set them free. The more truth they receive, the more freedom they receive and the more freedom they receive, the more attractive they are to those bound in fear.

Do you long for His presence in your life?

Conditions of Acceptance

WEEK 10

Read John 4:43-53

In last week's devotion we looked at how the Samaritan people came to know Jesus. Not once did they ask to see any signs or wonders, they heard the testimony of the woman and spent time in Jesus' presence. The text said that they begged Him to stay longer. That's a heart of someone that God can work in – longing after His presence not His presents.

They say this about children too, don't they? As parenting advice goes, we are told not to 'spoil' our children. We see those who are showered in gifts and material positions only grow to want more and more. Those possessions will never make up for a lifetime of loneliness. A feeling I know all too well. I believe that our presence for our children is by far more important to their lives, the same goes for God.

When Jesus embarked on His journey to Galilee where He was raised, He had a perception of what He might face there. The text tells us that prophets were honoured everywhere they go; anywhere except their hometown. We see that He was in fact welcomed by the people there, possibly because they had seen the miracles He performed during Passover. As He entered the village of Cana there was a government official who had made the journey there especially because he knew Jesus would be there. His son was sick, and this was a mercy mission of around 20 miles on foot.

The official, probably on his knees in front of Jesus, begs Him to go with him and save his son. Jesus' response is an interesting one. This response gives me grounds to suggest that some of us may be longing for presents, not presence.

Jesus knew that He would be rejected here. His response was almost a criticism in the sense of exasperation: 'You people never believe unless you see signs and wonders.' We need to bear in mind where Jesus had come from. The people in the Samaritan village were so hungry for His teaching. He then comes to a place where again He must prove Himself. These people were the counter opposite and they had conditions of acceptance that would apply to their faith in Jesus.

How often do we ask God to show us signs and wonders before we move? The woman at the well moved although she was confused.

Over the weeks so far I've shared parts of my story with you and I, too, wanted to see signs and wonders before I was fully in for Jesus. I spent so long asking for them that I was missing the ones in front of me. How many of us know that God is at work *all* of the time? If we know that then why are we so fixated on the one sign? Jesus asks us to follow Him, to live by faith not by sight. That involves actually not knowing what He is doing. We have to trust Him fully, surrendered to His will even though we don't know how that may pan out.

Despite Jesus' comment, the man continues to plead with Jesus for His intervention a second time. Jesus' response: He tells Him to go home NOW. This man had a choice. In the beginning he had asked Jesus to go with him to heal his son; he could have stayed and pleaded for Jesus to go with him or he could follow the advice of Jesus: 'Go now, your son will be healed.'

I wonder how differently the story would have turned out had the man continued to plead. Would he have lost his son in the demand of having his own way?

Thankfully, the text tells us: the man believed in his heart that what Jesus said is done was done.

I'd like to spend some time this week thinking about what we are asking Jesus for.

What miracle's in your life are you wanting Him to perform?

This man followed the instruction of Jesus and went back to his son. His request fulfilled and his son healed. But what if he hadn't done that? What if halfway home he was filled with doubt and turned back to plead with Jesus again?

We do that. We ask Jesus to work out something in our lives, we begin by following His instruction but then for some reason, in my case usually fear, we turn on our heels and go another way.

What if the man gave Jesus a deadline?

If his servant didn't come to him at the time specified, he turned back to yell at Jesus and allow his doubt to fill him with resentment.

We do that too. We take the instruction but then we give Jesus a time frame for us to see fruit from whatever it is we are doing: if this doesn't happen by this specific time I'm giving up. I shared with you a story about a lady who continued to pray for me as child; she didn't cease. She had no idea where I was or even if I was still alive, she just prayed because that's what God told her to. What if she gave up?

We seem to give Jesus these conditions of acceptance in order to prompt Him to go to work. Yet we neglect to carry out the instructions He gives to us.

What has Jesus asked you to do?

The story is one of a happy ending. Halfway home the man was met by one of his servants to inform him his son was well. Jesus didn't make him walk all the way to find out.

That's the thing with obedience. As we walk it out, we will see those blessings come. He tells us later (John 14:12-14) that if we follow Him in faith, whatever we ask in His name will be done. We must believe in our hearts that it is so. Proverbs 23:7 in the King James Version tells us, 'As he thinketh in his heart so is he.' Believing in our hearts is all about faith and faith is believing in the unseen. We can't place conditions in the contract when we surrender our lives to the Lord. If our minds are filled with fear and doubt our hearts will become hardened, our expectancy fades and we end feeling lost and defeated. Faith is a muscle that must be exercised regularly to keep our hearts in shape.

Maybe you're facing a situation right now that you can't see any hope in. I pray that this portion of scripture speaks life into it and that you can give to Jesus and believe in your heart that He will work it out for your good (see Romans 8:28).

What will the situation you've given to Jesus and walking out His instructions with belief in your heart look like?

Stinking Thinking

WEEK 11

Read John 5:1-16

After healing the son of the government official due to his faith and obedience, Jesus heads off to Jerusalem to observe one of the Jewish holy days. The text doesn't mention which and neither does it suggest there was anyone with Him. As He enters the city, we see Him walk by a pool. The pool is called 'The House of Loving Kindness' according to the notes in The Passion Translation. We see that this pool is covered by five porches. Upon delving into the notes of The Passion Translation it suggests that these five porches can represent the first five books of the Torah, the law, which is poignant, I think, to those lying under it.

These people would have been the outcasts of society of this day. The belief was that any disability caused to people from birth or beyond was as a result of sin. The religious leaders were elite and classed themselves as closer to God than anyone else and separated from sin so those seen as sinful, as we've seen over the weeks, are cast away and never to be spoken of again.

Legalism and religion can be like that. When we are striving to keep to rules and regulations its hard, it becomes a duty. So much so that we isolate ourselves and come under a porch which is dark and lonely. That's exactly the position the devil wants us to be in: alone, full of fear and striving to do something that is unreachable. That's the perfect place for him to attack our mind. When we are alone and set apart from other parts of the body, we become vulnerable to him and that's when his voice is the loudest.

Here we see a man completely opposite to the one we looked at last week. His mindset was one that was already defeated. He saw no hope and lay by that pool filled with apathy. This man wasn't a well-to-do official. He was a nobody cast out from civilisation and left alone to die. He had no money, no status, no authority – just his own thoughts and the resentment of not being able to get to the pool in time for his healing. The similarity we begin to see, though, is the compassion of Jesus. Despite the differences in the two men requiring miracles, Jesus moves with the same compassion to help them.

Jesus asked him, 'Do you truly long to be healed?'

I think this question was like the one He asked to me at the beginning of my journey with Him. Did this man really long to be healed? Of course he did! Although, he had given up and he had allowed the enemy to rob him of any hope he had of becoming complete.

What does it mean to truly long for something? How do we behave? I think that if I truly long for something I'll find a way to make it happen. If I put all of my hope in the One who died for me to come to life, then how can I fail? The problem was that this man had become spiritually paralysed as well as physically. He replied to Jesus, 'There is no way I can get healed.' He had succumbed to the fact that he would lie there for the rest of his days.

What are you truly longing for?

He then went on to inform Jesus that he had no one to take him to the pool. His healing depended on having someone to help him. Again, this prompts me to think about my own issues. Do I depend on others to lead me to the source of deliverance?

For years now I've felt God ask me to speak. I love to teach the Word of God and I love the freedom people find from His truth, but it has been something I've battled with for a long time. I analyse it all the time; I don't want it to be flesh desiring to speak and self-promotion is something I fear people thinking of me. The devil knows this and continually taunts me with it. It's been just as much of a battle to write this book. 'Who do I think I am?'

For ages I asked God to allow someone to speak into my life to confirm it. I'm still waiting for that prophecy to be spoken over me. Now, does that mean that He hasn't called me? I don't think so.

God is the only one who confirms my identity and He has confirmed that this is something He is asking me to do. But first I need to go on a journey with Him. I've seen many others be prophesied over and wondered why they aren't prophesying over me. I've asked for it but this all comes down to the root I've already disclosed to you. Fear of rejection. To be free of this I need to stop relying on the people around me to approve me.

What I've learnt is, in order to speak truth, I have to learn the truth. The way to learn is to see and experience. If my calling is affirmed by man, then I will continually turn to man to be approved. If I'm turning to man, I'm not turning to Jesus. The more I learn, the more I feel prepared and become less concerned with when that will be or what people think.

Are you relying upon anyone other than God for your blessing?

The next thing the paralysed man goes on to say is, 'When I have tried someone gets there before me.'

I've feared that too. What if someone steps up to this calling and I miss it? This is yet another example of the fear of rejection I hold in my life. If my identity is in the truth that God speaks over my life, He says I'm unique. There is only one me. He planned me before the beginning of time. If that is so, God looked at this grand universe and thought, 'I need to place a Rachael right there.' If there's no coincidence I'm here and the desires of my heart are planted by God, then how can anyone get to where He planned me to go?

We are so busy comparing ourselves, looking at others, that we miss what God has for us.

Everything about this guy's thinking was negative. Don't get me wrong, I can see why. In his mind everything was against him. But we are called to live by faith not by sight, and the promise of God tells us that we can do all things through Christ who strengthens us.

The message that this story gives to me is that it all starts with what we are thinking. We have to fill our heart and our head with the truth. Despite this man's negativity Jesus healed him, but for 38 years this man lay in waiting, dependent on the ideal circumstances.

What circumstances are you depending on?

For Whose Glory?

WEEK 12

Read John 5:17-24

Last week we looked at how our thinking affects our actions, which in turn affects the outcome of our circumstances. This week we are going to look at Jesus' response to the religious leaders after the healing of the man at Bethesda. The leaders instantly persecuted Jesus because the healing took place on the Sabbath but, as we well know, that wasn't the root reason of the persecution. No matter what Jesus had done, they were desperate to take Him out.

The first thing to come out of Jesus' mouth infuriated them. According to the text they were angry not only that He had broken the Sabbath rules, but He was now relating to God as 'My Father', which made Him equal to God! We know that they were the only ones they saw being unseparated from the Father.

This got me thinking about how we sometimes do and say things that are just going to irritate people. Unintentionally we go about our day doing what we think is right and for some reason, completely unbeknown to us, we get a backlash from someone who's just frustrated. Although that frustration might not actually be our fault, we are the person they choose to take it out on! Do you ever get that or am I on my own here?

Clearly Jesus knew why these people were infuriated in the context of this portion of scripture, but I believe that we can learn here how to deal with similar opposition from reading how Jesus responds. But before we dig in, I want you to take out your journal and ponder this question for our 'Reflect' area of today's devotion:

Can you think of a time when you were on the receiving end of someone else's frustration?

We see in Jesus' response straight away that He points to His Father, God. This is a great way for us also to check ourselves when we are in these situations. Sometimes it could be that we've been a bit thoughtless and said the wrong thing. Other times it could be that something we are doing is irritating something that is going on inside that person and that's through no fault of our own. Whichever it is, I find it useful to look to myself when I'm on the receiving end of someone else's frustration.

What was I doing or saying that caused them to react the way that they did to me?

Was I pointing to God or away from God?

What was the motive?

Jesus tells His critics that He can do nothing through His own initiative. So, all that He does, He does because He sees the Father doing it.

I think that the key here is knowing the heart of God. He's the creator of the heavens and the earth, everything that lives and breathes He designed. And He designed us in His image, and His Son's image and the Holy Spirit's image. So effectively, apart from Him we, too, can only do what we see Him doing. But, then there's the whole issue of freewill and the fall again, isn't there? We get to decide what's right and what's wrong. In order to learn what we do as His image bearers we need to know Him fully, just as Jesus describes in today's portion of scripture.

Although, knowing God in this depth might not take away tension that other people have against us. In fact, in some cases it may make it worse but knowing whose image we carry and our motive being glorifying to God will be the clincher in the way that we deal with it.

There have been many times, still are and will probably be more to come, where I've reacted or responded in a way that certainly does not glorify God. I'm reliant upon the grace of God, the leading of the Holy Spirit and my relationship with Jesus to understand the reasoning behind my behaviour. With that combined I know that I'm a work in progress. Times where I am persecuted, I have a benchmark to check myself with.

Here's another benchmark we can use: 'Because the Father loves his Son so much, he always reveals to me everything he is about to do' (John 5:20).

That's the relationship I want with my Papa!

A few months ago, I went for some prayer ministry called Sozo, originating from Bethel. It's an amazing ministry that is peaceful, honouring and empowering. It allows you to connect with Father God, Jesus and Holy Spirit regarding issues that might be holding you back from your relationship with them. It's like nothing I've experienced before. In the meeting you are encouraged to speak to Father, Jesus and Holy Spirit and wait for them to respond to you. There are two people in the room: one leads you to ask questions to each member of the Godhead and the other writes down all the truths that you hear. By the end of the meeting you have a love letter in your hand. It really is beautiful.

At that time, I had some real issues again to do with the root I battle most with: rejection. The truth I walked out of the room with that day literally had me in tears for weeks. It is a time that I will continue to go back to over and over. That day taught me that God is always ready to speak when we are ready to listen. I think sometimes we are waiting for a booming voice to come in a clap of thunder and a bolt of lightning, to actually believe that God is speaking to us. We fear our own thoughts and mindsets. We overthink and deny that some things we hear in our hearts are in fact God speaking to us.

Since that day, I regularly spend time asking God, Jesus and the Holy Spirit to talk to me. They regularly input into my life regarding situations around me and prompt me in solutions to problems I'm facing. I journal down what I hear, then pray and ask them to direct me to a word in the Bible to confirm all they've said. I might not get the Bible verses straight away or they may come in forms of devotionals like this one. But I can assure you that I've never not received confirmation on what God is speaking into my life. If it's true, noble, right, pure, lovely, admirable, excellent or praiseworthy we are hearing from God (Philippians 4:8).

When was the last time you stopped, asked God for His truth and allowed God to speak over you?

In the final verse of this week's study portion Jesus tells us that if we embrace His message and believe in the One who sent Him, we will never face condemnation. He goes on to say that by doing so we have passed from the realm of death into the realm of eternal life!

There it is! In Him we are living and will live eternally. Now. No matter what the outward world looks like we have eternal life that begins the moment we accept Him to live within us.

Do you feel like that right now?

No matter who is persecuting you, how you feel, what's happened at work, what mistakes you've made lately, there is no condemnation (Romans 8:1).

We passed through the realm of death. No matter what you are going through it is not your reality. The reality is in this portion of scripture. You are in Christ, He is in you, He is in the Father, and you have been raised to eternal life. NOW.

Ask Father God, Jesus and the Holy Spirit for some truth to journal out for the last question of today's devotion.

Arise with Life

WEEK 13

Read John 5:25-32

In this week's portion of scripture Jesus talks to the people about the two resurrections. His opening statement describes what will happen when the dead will hear His voice, but in the latter part of that verse He says that those who listen will arise with life.

Last week we talked about what happens when we listen to unprovoked criticism. We learnt that to be confident in who we are we first need to know the One who created us. Here we see again that in order to receive life we need to listen. Listen with such intent that we understand the voice of our Saviour. The very core of life itself. The authority to judge is given by the Father into Jesus' hands, therefore the only person who we should listen to regarding our actions on this earth is Him. We also spent some time last week listening out for the voice of God and journaled that down.

How did that feel for you?

When I find I'm battling with anything at all, the first thing I do is get out my journal and get it all off my mind. That's where the 'Remove' step of this study came from. I find that in order to hear the voice of Jesus I need to have less noise in my mind.

Admittedly, it does feel a bit weird at first, maybe a little childlike, but I can honestly say I've had so much revelation by doing so. The next step is reflection. Whether it's in the context of devotional reflection like this or just waiting on God and writing down what you think the Holy Spirit is saying, it's powerful stuff. I always find I get an answer. But the key is to listen, and first remove thoughts that are worldly.

Jesus goes on to tell the critics that there's a day coming when all who have died will hear His voice and rise from the grave. Those who have done good will be resurrected to eternal life and those who have practised evil will taste the resurrection that brings them to condemnation. Now, let's think about the life we are in now regarding this context. We have looked in previous devotions at the possibility of perishing here on earth and not living our best life. The one that Jesus died to allow us to have. But let us really look at the world we live in and ask ourselves, are people living in the grave but yet breathing? I think so.

Not long ago my husband and I attended the funeral of a friend he was close to in his young adulthood. It made me reflect a lot on life itself and the life that we could be living without Jesus. I found myself thinking about all the things I'd been set free from and how when those burdens are held in, we wither inside. Not just emotionally or spiritually but physically too. I found myself thinking about people I knew who still didn't know the freedom of Christ and how they were holding on to bitterness from circumstances the world had provided them with. Then I realised that most of these people, if not all of them, had some or many forms of physical illness that stopped them from doing the things that they desired to do. There are many people who reach the end of their lives and realise just how much they haven't lived at all. To me that's someone in a grave. Breathing or not.

How can you ensure that you are living to the best of your ability today?

Jesus goes on to explain that He is given the judgement from His Father to execute; nothing He does is of His own initiative; He only fulfils the Father's desires. That says a lot for Him bringing us life, doesn't it? It's God's desire for us to live, fully, abundantly free, in peace, with joy and justice. He wants us out of the grave and wholly alive.

I don't know about you, but I grew up thinking that God was a tyrant on a cloud somewhere frowning upon my bad behaviour and attitude of entitlement. I don't think I ever believed He loved me the way that the Bible describes. That's obviously because I was never taught to read the Bible or the truth from it. It's also because I felt my earthly relationship with my dad was one of disappointment. I always felt that I was a huge disappointment to him and never actually did anything to make him proud of me. In my teenage years I actually grew to resent that relationship. I blamed him, along with others, for a lot of things that went wrong in my life, and some poor decisions I believe I made because I felt like I was such a let-down and so unloved.

As I matured into early adulthood the resentment started to reduce a little bit, but I still felt unloved and made as many wrong decisions as I did in my teenage years. Then I met Jesus, and it changed totally for me. I began to see things from a totally different perspective. As I realised it wasn't my parents' fault for the way my life turned out I began to resent the circumstances rather than their choices. It wasn't their fault they were forced into the choices they were, just as much as it wasn't my fault. Yes, we made errors. Yes, some of those decisions were downright stupid. But what lay beneath were the reasons behind those choices. A lifetime of events that impacted our lives and had us believe a lie that resulted in the wrong decisions being made. It's never actually the people that are bad. I began to think like Jesus. A new way of thinking enabled me to judge people less and recognise which battle to choose. I began to execute judgement based on the principals of the Father who loved me rather than the circumstances that influenced my life.

Are there any situations that you could judge differently?

Man's Approval

WEEK 14

Read John 5:33-47

This week Jesus continues His response to the religious leaders who are gunning for Him for healing on the Sabbath. Jesus goes on to tell them that the approval of man is something He certainly doesn't need. His words are not to please them but to free them from the oppression of religion.

Thinking about this in the modern day, I think we can all agree that via the internet and social media we are indeed more connected to people across the globe than ever. So much so that people read about an earthquake on Twitter minutes before feeling the tremor! As useful as this technology can be, it's also a curse. I dread to think how many hours I spend mindlessly scrolling through my social newsfeeds. Consuming hundreds of selfies that are enhanced by filters or comparing my parenting to the posts of the perfect family. Some days I might actually post something, and I find I'm defining myself by the number of likes of comments I get. It's such a comparison trap!

Before long I find my mind is consumed and I'm defined by the approval of man. Unfortunately, this only adds to our insecurities, it's hindering our freedom and keeping us bound up in fear. Why on earth would we do such a thing? As I scroll and find myself falling into the trap, I'll hear a voice within me: 'Rachael, it's time to stop. You are not defined by these things and you need to embrace the One we are defined by.'

Are there any areas of your life you feel you need to be defined by the approval of others?

Jesus goes on to inform His opponents of the testimonies that prove who He is. Now, there is some context to this. According to the law of Moses a man's testimony about himself is inadmissible. Jesus is stating the facts here. Not only is He His own witness, John is, the Father is, His miracles are, and scripture is. There is no mistake: He is who He says He is!

Jesus tells the men:

'You are busy analysing the Scriptures, frantically poring over them in hopes of gaining eternal life. Everything you read points to me, yet you still refuse to come to me so I can give you the life you're looking for – eternal life!' (John 5:39-40)

What a statement. These men are so consumed with filling their heads with knowledge they've totally missed the lesson. I find that happens to me at times. It's called pride, I think.

I can always tell when I'm being proud; it comes with impatience. I'll be listening to someone talk and find that I'm waiting for them to finish so I can boastfully inform them of what I know!

First pride, then the crash – the bigger the ego, the harder the fall. (Proverbs 16:18 MSG)

When I became a Christian, I used to think that if I analysed the Bible and became more knowledgeable, I'd be able to have intelligent conversations with those I felt inferior to.

The problem was, the more I read the more I began to think I knew it all! I would find myself boastfully throwing around my knowledge. I soon crashed and fell. Doing things this way isn't growing in a relationship. It's religion, and I was no better than these Pharisees. Even worse, I sounded like a younger version of Dot Cotton from *EastEnders* constantly firing out mindless scriptures all over the place!

I think we will all agree that's not what we use the Bible for. Here we see it confirmed by Jesus Himself. To study the Word is to grow in our relationship with the Father, to commune with Him and discover for ourselves His heart, the nature of His son and the role of the Son and Holy Spirit in our lives. So, let's reflect on this next question:

How has your study time influenced your relationship with Jesus?

The last part of today's portion really hits home for me. Jesus tells them that He does not accept the honour that comes from men. Particularly these men, because they refused to embrace Him and His message. He knew that His Father's love was not in their hearts. Yet they embraced the message of those that claimed to be elite.

The thought that struck me as I read was, this is how Jesus feels when I reject my alone time with Him to please someone who I think is important. That maybe a boss, a leader, a parent I envy, but the root reason for following them is to get some sort of approval or status. I think it's a cycle we can all say we've been caught up in.

I used to be a sales manager for a large IT corporation. The best way to get a promotion in that place was to please those in higher ranks. There were so many underhanded things that went on it was beyond belief. After going on maternity leave to have my first son I soon realised the fragility of life. I decided that the career I once enjoyed was something I couldn't return to. I pottered around doing different types of jobs in the next 18 months and found that I just couldn't settle; there was more I wanted from life and I wouldn't settle until I found it. So, whilst on maternity leave after having my second son, I decided to set up my own business. I was a talented salesperson and knew that was something most small businesses lacked. So I started to work for smaller companies to do their cold calling for them. I knew this was something many single business owners struggled with so it wasn't hard to find customers. Before long I'd grown my reputation and met regularly with other business owners at networking meetings. Again, I saw the cycle of comparison and pride return. I started working with some high-profile people and before long was coveting their success and I wouldn't stop until I had it. This was at the sacrifice of my marriage and my family. I'd spend less time at home and when I was there, I'd be busily working away in my office. My husband and I would drink heavily and argue – a lot! Then the depression started to seep in; I'd feel worthless and rejected in my attempt to make the cut and be noticed but most of all I became burnt out. It was hard work living a lie. That's when we found Jesus and it all began to become clear. I recognised that this cycle was repeated through my life and it was down to a root fear of rejection. I longed to be liked and worthy of praise. So, I continually strived in my own strength to get what I thought would make me this way.

The only way to acceptance is through Jesus. When we discover who He is and what He came to achieve, we discover who the Father is and why He created us. When God's love for us becomes tangible and real we see who we are. If we chose to accept Jesus and be filled with the Holy Spirit, we can then identify how to navigate life as He knows it, not as the world knows it.

The Pharisees had no idea who God was. Right there before them stood the One they had spent their lives waiting for, but they were so blinded by holding on to their authority over the people they missed it completely.

The last question to ponder for this week is about you:

Can you see any cycles in your life that might indicate you don't accept yourself through Jesus?

Be Still and Know

WEEK 15

Read John 6:1-15

This week we are looking at another great miracle in John chapter 6. Throughout Jesus' ministry we discover that He is continually showing and teaching His disciples *how* to do things and this week we witness a little test for Philip! Jesus asks Philip *where* will we buy enough food? He didn't ask *how* we will buy enough food. Straight away Philip begins to think logically. Despite the miracles he's already seen, Philip begins by thinking about the problem; in his mind at that moment he couldn't see how they would feed all those people and the responsibility was on his shoulders.

This makes me think of us when we face problems in our lives. Although we've seen how Jesus has changed our lives, we've encountered miraculous wonders, received supernatural strength in situations beyond our control and have felt the touch of the Holy Spirit, and yet there are times when we can't quite look to Jesus to meet our needs or we struggle to perceive the concept of miracles. We take on the burden for ourselves and conclude that *we* must sort it out. *We still lack that faith at times.*

Naturally, the first thing we do when we have a problem is to panic about it. We weigh up how we might solve it in the flesh; it's not instinctive to take that problem to Jesus. I wonder why that is? I know from my own life that when I'm so full up on the Word of God I feel like anything is possible. I walk with confidence knowing that my creator is for me and no matter what I face He will go to work on my behalf. I've seen it happen. I need only be still. Is that the stance I take when trouble comes, though? No, not initially. My initial stance is to defend, fight or flight. It's a process. Once I'm over the initial shock of whatever the circumstance might be, I look up. I ask Jesus to intervene.

My first question for you to ponder today is:

What's your initial stance?

Who we look to and how we respond is something we need to continually keep a check on.

Next it's Andrew's turn to be tested. A young boy comes from the crowd with all he has to help feed everyone, yet Andrew questions whether it's enough. Again, this is something we grapple with in the midst of a storm. Will Jesus provide enough? Whilst going through the finances we question how on earth we will make ends meet, how can Jesus get us enough to provide? Yet He always does.

A couple of years ago, my husband and I began training on a leadership course; we didn't really have the time or the finance to pay for it but we felt that it was something God wanted us to do. We had a 9-month-old baby, two other boys to feed, a business that was in its infancy and wondered how on earth we would pay for both of us to do the course. Not only that, there was the time we needed to dedicate to doing the course. We also had to pay for a week's mission. We had two choices in the midst of this: worry or trust that Jesus would provide. We did both! The money came and the time appeared. If I did it again would I scrap the worry? Probably not. I think it's all part of the lesson.

I do wonder, did this young boy know exactly who Jesus was? I find it quite the coincidence that the Bible tells us to come to Him like children and here we have a child coming forward with all he has, allowing Jesus to multiply! What happens next is a great example of what happens when you bring all you have to Him. When we give of ourselves, Jesus will take what we have and multiply it. The leadership course we did was not only paid for in full by the end of it but we found time we didn't know we had, our business grew despite us not being in it and our relationship with Jesus grew. In trusting Him and giving of ourselves we saw multiplication.

What can you give of yourself?

Sometimes we think that we need to work harder in order to bring more to Jesus. I don't believe that. Yes, my husband and I worked harder to do the leadership course, but we did it to the rhythm of the Holy Spirit. We prayed about doing the course and God gave us a firm 'yes'. We knew that by following His will we would have the strength to accomplish what was being asked of us. I don't believe that we have to strive and work harder unnecessarily to see God move. In this testimony my husband and I were 'still' before God in our decision to move. It's not about working harder to gain more, it's about prayerfully considering where God wants you to give of yourself. I hear the phrase 'get up and work for it' a lot. And whilst I agree we need to work towards goals, I disagree that we need to strive; there needs to be balance, and prayerful balance at that.

The first thing Jesus did when He provided for over 5000 people was have them sit down. The Bible tells us that 5000 men were fed that day, it didn't include their families so there were more than 5000 people there. I can imagine it was complete chaos, people clambering over one another to catch a glimpse of Him, but Jesus wanted peace and order. He wanted them sitting down, still and patient. He wanted them to see what He was about to do because there was a big lesson to be learnt.

A lesson He wanted them to take away with them. A lesson He wants us to learn also. We don't have to strive to work harder to receive His blessing. Jesus wants us to SIT and RECEIVE, REST and RECEIVE, BE STILL and RECEIVE.

Jesus teaches us in this small portion of scripture exactly how to live a life of abundant peace.

1. Bring what you have
2. Be still
3. Look up
4. Give thanks
5. Receive

It really is that simple. This young boy came and gave what He had to Jesus for Him to use for the good of others. It wasn't much and I believe that was intentional. We don't have to be breaking our necks – working hard, giving hard – but we do need to humbly bring what we have to Jesus. Our time, finance, resources . . . whatever the Holy Spirit prompts you to bring. We lift that up to God, look up and give thanks for what we have, not reflecting on what we don't have. We then rest in His presence and receive the multiplication.

The decision to be still in the midst of chaos will result in peace and order. We don't have to strive and stress about the solution, we just need to remember what the little boy did. He brought what He had to Jesus and allowed Him to do the rest. The final question for today to journal out as we reflect on this portion of scripture is:

When was the last time you were still before Jesus?

It's in the Waiting

WEEK 16

Read John 6:13-21

This week we are looking at what it means to wait for something. I don't know about you but I'm not a very patient person, although my household constantly tests me on this and I'm starting to improve. My middle son is the most laid-back person I've ever met. Whilst waiting for him to complete tasks I'm always reminded of what it means to be patient; he doesn't rush for anyone! Although those times of waiting require patience, I'd like to think of more pressing things we are waiting for on our journey of faith.

As I think about this, I recall the beginning of my journey. Over the weeks I've talked a lot about this but in the beginning I felt that I was a no-hoper, someone beyond help. I'd see the people around me filled with hope and joy and wonder what it was like to live in their world. I'd hear testimony after testimony of restoration and long to receive that for me, and the more I longed the angrier and more bitter I became. I wasn't waiting well at all.

In the portion of scripture we are reading today we see the disciples doing a little bit of waiting of their own. We pick up this story right after Jesus had just fed 5000 men and their families from a couple of bits of fish and bread. Consider and imagine how the disciples were feeling, left hanging around after all this excitement of seeing Jesus perform this amazing miracle. Maybe they were reflecting on their own thoughts, processing what had just happened and probably feeling very excited and expectant for what will happen next. But as they wait the thoughts continue to mull around in their mind. They get to thinking about who they are, who they're not, what they can and can't do, why they are there, what they are waiting for . . . the list goes on. That's the thing with thinking, without warning it can spiral into something that limits our faith. I think that's why the Bible tells us to renew our mind.

Waiting is something we will all have to do continually throughout our lifetime. We have hopes for our lives and those hopes are normally something that we have to wait for. It could be waiting for a man to marry, to conceive a child, for a ministry to birth, for a new job to come, for a new house, for a change in financial circumstance, for an illness to be healed, for a relationship to be restored – whatever it is we have to wait well. We are all waiting on something, so the first question today is:

What are you waiting for?

In my experience of waiting I know that we have the ability to grow.

From what I can see from this wonderful story and also in my own times of waiting is that it is in the waiting that we experience huge growth. God says I want you to have this thing you are waiting for but I'm not about to give it to you on a plate. We have to continue to go through a process of refining. As He refines us, we navigate storms of all varieties as the disciples did this day on the boat.

It's in the storm that we learn resilience, it's in the storm that we discover how strong we can be, it's in the storm we recognise the areas we need to develop.

The disciples discover in this story that their area of development needed to be a little more faith. In the two other accounts we see Peter step out in that addition of faith quite literally: he trusts Jesus and takes hold of His hand to walk on the water, but in the split second he takes his eyes off Jesus, he begins to sink.

In the storm we learn so much, BUT only *if* we allow . . .

There are many different ways in which we deal with waiting and here are three I can think of that I've seen in my own life.

We could strive and push in our own strength, setting unattainable goals and challenging ourselves to breaking point in the mindset of, 'If I want it, I must go out and get it.' This person would be so busy, they don't have time to be still and allow God to speak. They would continually be pushing on doors that have closed and be totally determined that they are right and the things against them are wrong.

We could give in and stop and let go of the promise we've been waiting for. This person would be someone that's fed up and burnt out, possibly as a result of continually pushing against God's will. They've not had time to rest in God so therefore have lost focus of His promise and come to the conclusion they are barking up the wrong tree. So, they give up completely or, worse, they are completely exhausted and have been made to give up.

Or we could do it the way Jesus wants us to. We could be still and peaceful, resting in faith that the promise will come to pass. This person would continue to worship and praise God in the storm, be rooted in the Word and speak life continually into their problems.

The next question I want you to ponder on is:

What do you do in the waiting?

Do any of the above resonate or do you imagine any of your own descriptions?

The fact of the matter is that Jesus came and spoke to the storm. Despite the faithless reaction of the disciples, Jesus came and calmed that storm, the winds and waves were no more, and peace was restored. This is what He will do for us if we choose to recognise it; every season of our lives is an opportunity to learn, be stretched and grow, but without the storm in the waiting, we won't grow.

Have you ever seen a child who is given everything they ask for without question? We generally call them spoilt. The fact is we are spoilt too; we are a fallen humanity, spoiled with sin. God wants us to learn where those weak spots are and, to do that, He has to allow us waiting and, in the waiting, we are tested by the storms.

God wants to teach us to navigate these life storms, He wants us to sail through and grow whilst on the move. This is the reason Jesus gave us His living church to attend. The sermon we hear on a Sunday isn't just a speech, it's the living, breathing Word direct from the mouth of God. He doesn't want us to just sit and listen to it, He wants us to WAIT in it, ACT upon it, STUDY it, PLANT it firmly in our hearts in order to GROW, in order that we might navigate those high winds and waves, as the experienced sailors He ordained us to be!

What truth can you speak in times of your storm?

Requirements of Faith

WEEK 17

Read John 6:21-31

This week we are going to look at the reactions of the people following the miracle of feeding the 5000 and how their requirements of Jesus in order to ignite their faith were something that we, too, can sometimes have.

The morning after the night before the people searched for Jesus and He was nowhere to be found. They went off to find Him and when they did, they asked how He had gotten there. They were confused because there had only been one boat that the disciples boarded without Jesus, so couldn't figure how He had travelled over the lake. His concern was *why* they were following Him. They didn't follow Him with a desire to know who He was. They didn't want to know how this would impact the world. They didn't even care what it was He had come to do. They were mesmerised by the miracle. In week 3 we looked at His question to the disciples: 'What do you want?' Jesus didn't need to ask the people what they wanted here. He knew. They wanted more miracles.

Again, it makes me wonder what requiremonts we have in order to have faith. To grow in our relationship with Him, what is it we need to see? I know all too well what it's like in my life to be praying for something that seems to come back unanswered. Our youngest son suffers with a chest condition that affects his breathing, he has done since he was 9 months old and we have been in and out of hospital more times than I can remember. Many a night I've prayed and prayed for him to be well; in the early hours as he struggles to catch his breath, I've cried out asking for Jesus to open his airways and heal him, only to be going along to hospital an hour or so later. Does this deduct credit from my trust bank with Jesus? Yes, it does. I have questions about that, and I doubt His love for me as I'm sitting in the hospital waiting area watching all the other children suffering. But as we discussed last week, it's a storm that He is teaching me to navigate. The truth is I don't know why He hasn't performed the miracle I'm asking for but in the midst of that hospital trip I've seen Him at work. I've made friends with mums who don't know Him and some that do. I've had the opportunity to pray for people there, and maybe, just maybe, that prayer was answered. I just have to trust that there is a miracle somewhere in that circumstance. If I don't, I become like the Jews: demanding and unbelieving.

Are you waiting on a miracle to ignite your faith?

Jesus challenges the people regarding the type of food they come looking for. They want the perishable food that slides right through the digestive system. I imagine they are stood listening to Him, hungry again that morning because the food He provided the day before had gone, it was digested, and they needed more. As they stood before Him with pangs of hunger, He speaks of a nourishment that's beyond their understanding, a food that will never spoil, one that ignites passion and one that's eternal. It was there ready and waiting for them, all that they needed to do was to believe.

Because of the storms I've faced and those moments of doubt, I understand this eternal nourishment more now than I ever would have without them. It's ignited a passion within my heart to share this news with others. The desire in my heart is for all humanity to know about the freedom I have in Christ. That to live for Him is eternal life starting here and now. No matter what I face I have the One who created the heavens and the earth on my side. He loves me and there's hope even when it feels like there's none, despite it being beyond my comprehension.

Because of that passion I'm sitting writing these words in the hope that someone, somewhere, reads them and gains a better understanding of their ability to have a relationship with their creator. I can't begin to explain in the few words I write here but I'm a completely different person to who I was without Him. I understand what it is to be hungry and navigate this world without Him. So, with that in mind I focus on helping others to see the eternal promise which is available here and now. Maybe you feel the same.

Is there a passion that you have ignited in you through Jesus?

This portion of scripture follows a massive miracle. Yet we read through it the people asking to see signs and wonders in order to believe in Jesus. Wasn't it enough that He'd just fed over 5000 people with two pieces of fish and five loaves, let alone the rest of the miracles? These people were reliant upon seeing in order to believe.

Seeing is not believing. That is not the definition of faith. Second Corinthians 5:7 says, 'we live by faith not by sight'. Throughout this devotional I've talked a lot about my journey because I believe that it helps us to understand that the Word of God is not as estranged to life as we know it today. In the beginning of my walk I would ask, A LOT, for signs and wonders! I remember the day I crashed my car, driving along waiting for the sky to do something spectacular as I asked God to present Himself to me! It wasn't until much later as I reflected on that day, I saw the miracles.

The thing is, Jesus wants us to live a life filled with signs and wonders, but we can end up looking in the wrong places. We can get so distracted by our expectations that we miss what is going on before our eyes. We are co-partners with the creator, which means that we are to work with Him, not Him work with us. If we are dictating how it's going to look, we are taking His place as creator. We miss the relationship He so longs to have with us, and that is the ultimate miracle. The creator of everything we know, the One who controls the globe moving on its axis, who placed the stars in the sky, who created every single unique strand of DNA to form our existence wants an individual, loving relationship with me. WOW.

Let us reflect on that for a moment. Go somewhere quiet with your pen and journal and take some time to allow God to cover you in His love for the last question of today's devotional:

Ask God to tell you how He feels about you and write what you hear in the 'Reflect' section.

Daily Nourishment

WEEK 18

Read John 6:32-59

We left last week with the 5000 plus people who had been fed by two fish and five loaves asking Jesus for another miracle to help them with their lack of faith. In this week's portion of scripture He is trying to explain to them who He is and how they can be nourished with an eternal satisfaction. Jesus explains this perfectly along with advice we can take too. He says:

'I am the Bread of Life. Come every day to me and you will never be hungry. Believe in me and you will never be thirsty.'

My husband and I became Christians in a Pentecostal church that loved Jesus; they were amazing with us and we learnt very early on that you do not go a day without reading the Bible. If you miss a day spending time with Jesus, you'll go hungry. It's right, unless I spend time with Jesus I find I'm unfulfilled, there's something missing for that day. I'm not claiming I don't miss those times though; what I'm saying here is that when I do, I know there is something missing. Two of the fundamental things that we need as humans to survive are food and water, something that Jesus is telling the people here they will never lack. I know that when I have spent a good portion of my time with Jesus that I will face my day ahead full and satisfied.

Beginning a day this way radically changes the chances of it being a contented one or a frustrating one. If we begin our day with promise and purpose at the forefront, we can navigate the most irritating circumstances with peace and joy.

How do you feel when you've spent time with Jesus?

The Jews Jesus was speaking to didn't know what we do, they didn't get it at all. They began to grumble and turn on Him, wondering who on earth He thought He was. They were holding tightly to religion, legalism, power and authority. They had no desire at all to open their hearts to Him. The thought that maybe, just maybe, this man, son of Mary and Joseph, the carpenter, is the One who could change their lives, didn't even cross their minds.

We see this sort of persecution in the world today too. Those who have no knowledge of the Living Bread cling on to the crutches they've grown to love. I was the same. I held on to drink, drugs and indecent relationships because I had no idea of the truth. I didn't know what I didn't know. That was until God pulled on my heart to embrace Jesus, just as He describes in verse 43 of The Passion Translation.

The Jews had their eyes fixed on Moses. He was the one who delivered them from slavery, he sought God to provide for them and they idolised him for that. Those who stood in place of Moses were the religious leaders, the elite, those set apart from sin and closer to God than any other. But here stood a man who was explaining to them they could have a direct relationship with the Father through Him, which they couldn't comprehend.

Although we no longer live under religion and the law, I do still see that we look upon man to make things happen for us. We idolise celebrities, compare ourselves to people in church, at work and we compete with one another ending up bitter and frustrated. What if we lived in a world that accepted one another as individual and equal just as Jesus wants?

Growing up I idolised many people in my life. Mainly because I hated being me, I was caught in a trap of comparison and I'd do anything to be liked by those I compared myself to. I took up smoking at the age of 13 to be liked by girls I thought were better than me. That went on to be an addiction I struggle still now to break. I think back to all the ridiculous things I did to fit in and wonder what if I'd have known the truth sooner? The fact is, I didn't. The Bible tells us that God brings all things together for good. So, knowing the choices I made were wrong He is using me to help those who may feel the way that I did. Hopefully, my story might help that one person struggling to fit in, to recognise that he or she is made fearfully and wonderfully perfect just the way they are. My mistakes have formed part of my purpose.

What mistakes could you turn into purpose?

Jesus continues His explanation to the Jews and, as ever, is very controversial in His reasoning. He speaks of eating His flesh which is something that repulsed the people that were listening. It was forbidden by the law of Moses to drink blood of any kind, these words just infuriated them all the more. What we take from this portion of scripture is what it means to nourish ourselves in the truth. His flesh is the Word. We must yield ourselves to Him above all else. Without it we will perish, which is opposite to the eternal life Jesus described back in John 3:16. Now more than ever we need to be reminded of the truth in order to navigate a world of sin and distraction. We cannot live the life Jesus died to give us without the knowledge and wisdom we discover through the Holy Spirit by feeding from the Living Word of God. Our true identity is hidden there, and if we want to live on purpose, we have a responsibility to seek His will for our lives by continually pursuing His intention for us.

There is so much wisdom and knowledge in the world now that we tend to look up to people a lot. We value human opinions and approval, but we need to be alert and balance advice with the Word. We need to ensure that the opinions we collect are approved by the One who gave us our purpose in the first place. It's so important, now more than ever, that we discover who Jesus is and who we are in Him over everything.

How can you remind yourself of His truth regularly?

Mend the Fence

WEEK 19

Read John 6:60-70

After Jesus spoke about people eating of His body many of His disciples became offended and walked away – without actually understanding what Jesus meant they walked away. To eat meat that wasn't acceptable and drink blood was actually a violation of the law, this was the reasoning behind their offence. They were slaves to that law and didn't even entertain trying to grasp what Jesus could be teaching them; despite all they had seen and heard that encouraged them to follow Him, their response was to turn their back on Him immediately.

As I studied this portion of scripture, I began to think about how this looks in church. Unfortunately, offence in church is something that is unavoidable, no matter what we do we will always be offended or be the offender and, sadly, it is one of the main reasons people turn their backs on Jesus. It's the devil's favourite tactic: if he can have us offended with one another, he can initiate division.

One of the problems with offence is that often it isn't intentional. Usually, we find that we become offended by our interpretation of what was said or done. Because we are all created so uniquely, we all interpret things differently. What one person interprets from the words I write here will be interpreted in a different way to the next. It's the way of the world. But how can we navigate offence so that the conclusion isn't us turning away from the church? How can we be more empathetic towards one another and not have this turn into a divide?

In verse 63, Jesus begins to provide the answer. He said the Holy Spirit is the One who gives life, He's the comforter, the teacher and the nurturer. If we engage with Him, we will receive all that we need in order to fight away the upsetting words. His desire is for us to partner with Him rather than the lie we are believing about ourselves or the offending party. One of the gifts the Holy Spirit brings to us is discernment, and because we carry the Holy Spirit as part of our belief in Christ, we possess that gift, we can establish the root cause of offence. That may be a fear we are holding on to from our past that needs to be dealt with or it could be that the person we are offended by has a root in them that's initiated their thoughtless approach. Either way, the teacher is able to show us what we need to do in order to let it go.

There have been many times on my journey that I've been offended in church. I'd like to say that I've used the process of calling out to the Holy Spirit each time but that isn't true; I had to learn that's what I need to do before doing it. One thing that helped me to come to this conclusion was reading about the words Jesus spoke on the cross: 'Forgive them, for they know not what they do.' I began to think about it and realised that actually, when do people really know what their words or actions will initiate in others? Because we are all so different and are continually experiencing circumstances that determine our emotions, how can we know exactly why someone does or says what they do. What if they don't know the pain they are causing? What if the pain they are suffering is far greater than the pain I endure by their actions towards me? As I began to think this way, I found myself relying more and more on the Holy Spirit to lead me through these experiences and, as I did that, I discovered I became less and less offended.

Can you recall an offence that made you want to turn away?

It's painful when people turn away from us, isn't it? I imagine that Jesus felt the pain of this rejection too. He knows all too well what it's like to have people abandon you. The thing with offence is that it contaminates the heart. As we begin to partner with it, more lies appear and the offence grows, we begin to turn away from more people, those who love us dearly, and that's also painful for them to watch. In these times we instinctively want to run after those who are walking away, we want to fix it, but in reality, the only person who can fix it is Jesus. As we run after our friends and try to console them it can go two ways: we partner with their pain or we add to it. I've found that it's far easier to walk alongside them. To be there but not to fix. To point back to Jesus but not to partner with the pain.

I love this portion of scripture from Ephesians 4:1-6 in *The Message*:

> *In light of all this, here's what I want you to do. While I'm locked up here, a prisoner for the Master, I want you to get out there and walk – better yet, run! – on the road God called you to travel. I don't want any of you sitting around on your hands. I don't want anyone strolling off, down some path that goes nowhere. And mark that you do this with humility and discipline – not in fits and starts, but steadily, pouring yourselves out for each other in acts of love, alert at noticing differences and quick at mending fences.*
>
> *You were all called to travel on the same road and in the same direction, so stay together, both outwardly and inwardly. You have one Master, one faith, one baptism, one God and Father of all, who rules over all, works through all, and is present in all. Everything you are and think and do is permeated with Oneness.*

This portion of scripture speaks so well into this issue, it explains to me what to do for those struggling with offence around me too. So, my next question for us to reflect upon today is:

What stands out as you read Ephesians 4:1-6?

The last part of today's reading we see Peter confess his faith. Jesus turns to ask His chosen twelve if they will leave too. In the moment of Peter's confession, he hadn't realised he was chosen; it was after his declaration that Jesus replied with, 'I have hand-picked you to be my twelve, knowing that one of you is the devil' (John 6:70).

What a statement! It's like affirmation and rebuke all at once. I wonder what would have gone through my mind at hearing this. I'd certainly start to wonder who Jesus was referring to, then the thought process would wind up with me looking at my own heart and thinking He was referring to me being the devil! That's how Satan works though, isn't it? We hear something and along with it we hear a lie. Things like, they don't like you, you're rotten, you're a waste of space, worthless, proud, arrogant, whatever the recurring theme – mine is normally rooted in rejection. I'm not wanted, I'm not good enough, clever enough . . . the list is endless. This is why it's so important to renew our minds on a daily basis; we need to be consistent in speaking life over ourselves in order to stand firm in the anointing that Jesus has given us. We are hand-picked. Chosen. Called. Elected. Royal and dearly loved. We need to live as we are called. The slightest lie that we partner with has the ability to contaminate the heart. By attaching that lie to our lives we partner with the devil in his schemes and over time that partnering will bring down everything around us. If we are insecure in our identity, we become independent, proud, selfish, ambitious and we compete with those around us – this is not what we were hand-picked for.

My final question for today to reflect upon is:

What do you think God wants you to do next time you feel offended?

Which Direction?

WEEK 20

Read John 7:1-11

We read on to discover this week that Jesus continued to travel extensively. Today we look at the direction Jesus took in comparison to the direction people thought He should take. Jesus' brothers wanted Him to branch out; the reasoning was fame and fortune. Jesus teaches us in this portion what it is to be modest, which is not something that's easy to do in today's society. Jesus was firm in His response that the time for Him to be unveiled had not yet come, He then slipped away and travelled a back road so as not to be seen.

Looking at the world today it's hard to see modest behaviour, isn't it? We are judged upon appearance and status. We strive to be seen and teach our children to make something of their lives. As I've mentioned I grew up desperate to make my dad proud of me, so being modest wasn't something that came naturally to me. Naturally, we want to celebrate our achievements and do well for ourselves. I don't think that there is anything wrong with that, but I do believe that we have to continually check on our motive. Wanting to be well known and famous isn't a sin, but the reasoning behind that might be; are we honouring God in our ambitions?

In previous weeks I talked about a time in my life when I decided to set up a business. I was proud from the beginning if

I'm honest. Prior to setting up my business I'd worked on some projects with other small business owners, which is where I got the idea from: I thought, well if they can do it, I can do it, and I'll probably do a better job! I was going to make something of myself and everyone would know my name. It wasn't long before I started to get noticed and opportunities came my way. But there was a problem: imposter syndrome. Each time I attended a business networking meeting there would always be someone there who was better than me. Insecurity would strike and I'd come away feeling a fraud. Desperate to fight away these feelings I decided that the solution would be to spend £3995 on a diploma in marketing! It wasn't long before I realised I'd made a grave mistake. Part way through my studies I became a Christian and it wasn't long after giving my life to Jesus and allowing the Holy Spirit to fill me I heard a still small voice. I sensed that God was asking me to give up my business and work full time with my husband in his business. This would mean submitting myself to his dreams and ambitions and letting go of being the one at the forefront of our family's success. I'm ashamed to say that this is something I wrestled with . . . a lot. As I wrestled with God I began to see that my ambition and motive was wrong. It was something that grieved God and because of that wrongful motive I wasn't living the abundant peaceful life He wanted me to. As time went by, I wound down my company, I completed the diploma and settled into my new role as my husband's PA. I'm actually a partner in the business but I feel more like a PA! There's so much I learnt over that season of my life. I'd like to say that I've never chosen to do something with the wrong motive since but I'd be lying. However, I do recognise more easily when I am in the wrong and wrestle less on repenting from that.

The first question to ponder for today is:

What motives do you have for the desires you are striving to see fulfilled?

I read somewhere that you become like the five people you spend the most time with. I wonder what could have happened had Jesus allowed His brothers to influence Him. They clearly had bigger plans in their heart for Him. Sometimes in the world we find ourselves around people who influence our decisions, we mould ourselves and become more like them and find ourselves striving to meet their expectations so as to be accepted. Thankfully, Jesus knew that He needed to walk away from them in order to do what Father God was asking of Him. Maybe in your life at the moment there are some relationships that are causing you to walk in the wrong direction. Peer pressure is certainly something I can relate to. I'm sure you can, too. There are things that we do at times for the approval of others that are just plain toxic to the life that Jesus died for us to have. In order to deal with these issues, we need to evaluate our relationships and how they influence. It's good to note here that Jesus didn't sever the relationship, He just chose to walk another way. We don't necessarily need to cut people off, we just need to make a healthy choice in how they influence our lives.

So, in the next question to reflect on, ask the Holy Spirit to highlight this:

Are there some relationships you might need to introduce a healthy distance to?

Jesus told His brothers to go ahead and celebrate without Him. Again, I think that this gives us a good insight into what we should do with regards to relationships that might just be hindering our journey. He didn't rebuke them and point out their issues; despite knowing they didn't believe in Him as Saviour He told them to go on celebrating. Last week we talked about offence and having the ability to be empathetic towards people – their motive is their motive and although you might think it's wrong, they might not be ready to hear that. It's not our job to judge. We are responsible for our own heart and motive only.

Jesus knew that by going to Judea His life would be at risk. He knew that the expectation of His brothers wasn't what the Father wanted for Him, so He lingered behind and took a secret back road to get to the feast. It doesn't matter which road you take or the speed at which you take it, all that matters is you follow the will of God for your destination. By going at His pace, we are able to take in all the lessons and grow at just the right speed. What matters is that we identify the route God is showing us and the speed that He has set. Maybe you feel left behind, or the only one in front, but wherever you find yourself today it's always good practice to check in with the director.

The last question for today to pray over and reflect is:

Are you on the right road travelling at the right speed?

Controversy!

WEEK 21

Read John 7:12-36

In the next portion of scripture we see a differing of opinions amongst the people. I love how Jesus turned up to teach when the ceremony was almost over, He was certainly showing His brothers that He wouldn't be told by mere men what to do!

The differing of opinions here got me thinking about how different we all are in our beliefs, ethics and perspectives. What is really beautiful about church communities is the differences in the people that come together with one fundamental commonality: we all love Jesus. No matter what background we come from, what our profession, our financial status or qualification, we are all the same through the eyes of Jesus. Children of God. Designed by the creator for a unique purpose. But the picture here was not a representation of this. Sometimes in church this isn't the picture either.

Because we are all designed so differently things can look very different to us: what makes me tick doesn't make you tick, therefore there is a tension created when you try to explain to me something in which you desire to change. It takes a real empathy to understand one another in this area and, let's face it, it's hard work at times too. When we couple the difference of opinions with the insecurities we have and the root issues like rejection, in my case, it's a recipe for disaster. Insecurity makes you want to be heard; it makes you want to be right all of the time. So when it comes to listening to others what we hear isn't always what is said. Then the resulting feeling we carry isn't usually the truth. In order to eliminate this, we need to commit to actively listening to one another, not listening just to respond. If you find yourself listening to someone at the same time as preparing a response in your head, you aren't actively listening. This means that when this person is done it's likely you will give your response based on your opinion. If your response is to probe further into what the other is saying, this means that you are trying to further understand what they think, meaning you are genuinely trying to understand them. The result will be that they feel more valued and you will get a better perspective of what they feel and why they have that opinion.

The problem with the people here is that they had their opinion and they weren't budging. They had no time to listen to what Jesus was saying. When we really listen to one another we find we don't have a response lined up for when they have finished talking. When we don't have a response lined up, we release the ability to defend ourselves.

Let me give you an example of what this might look like in church today.

A group of ladies meet regularly; one of the ladies is passionate about people understanding their identity in Christ and creating events in order to create the environment for that to happen. Another is passionate about ladies on their own with children being loved and supported and knowing their identity in Christ. Unfortunately, the team that's available to make these events happen is small, which means that childcare isn't available. The lady who's passionate about single parents is immediately annoyed at this and is of the opinion that the single ladies are being excluded. The lady who's putting on the event is perplexed because she's doing her best. Neither lady is in the wrong, they just have a heart for different things. The solution here is for the ladies to come together and make the events happen WITH childcare, but the problem is neither party is listening to the other because they are focused on how their differing opinions make them feel.

So, my first question for today to reflect on is:

Is there an opinion you have heard lately that made you feel annoyed?

In verse 22 Jesus talks about the instruction of circumcision: if that fell on the Sabbath, they still had to carry out the ritual, which in effect breaks the law of the Sabbath. He used this as an example to embrace the standard of mercy and truth.

Mercy means to forgive, and to forgive we need to understand the heart of the person we are offering mercy to. To do so we need to be empathetic towards them. Using empathy to walk alongside people is something that will help us as we learn to navigate the abundant life Jesus died for us to have. As we begin to look upon things through the eyes of another, we find that we are loving people more like Jesus and are able to let go of any resentment we hold towards them. Jesus instructed people to stop judging on the superficial and that's what we are to do. So, with the opinion of another that made you feel annoyed I want to ask:

How can you change your perspective and see this opinion with empathy, through the eyes of the other person?

Following all the controversy, Jesus preached boldly about who He was and who sent Him. He pointed out again that the people knew nothing about His Father or His faithfulness towards them. Obviously they didn't understand, they only knew about the law. The character of God's loving nature was alien to them. Thankfully, we know that He is faithful, and His desire is to spend eternity with us. Even though we know this, lines still become blurred. As we try to reason with our life circumstances, we do often doubt his faithfulness. But unlike these people we have His Word, a lamp to light the way when we feel we don't know where we are going. When we pursue the truth and continue to nourish our hearts with His Word, we live in such a way that glorifies Him. Those of us who know Jesus and have encountered the faithfulness of God live differently to those who don't. There may be some of us who still doubt, but overall there's certainly something different about people who carry the Holy Spirit within, and that difference is attractive to those who don't know Him.

Life without Jesus is unthinkable to me now. My whole life has changed and it's more enjoyable because of His presence. My desire is for everyone I know to live this life but in order for that to happen and for me to reach these people I have to understand them. Sometimes, people persecute me for my belief and my love of Jesus. They may take a disliking to me because of the Spirit I carry within me. There have been times that I've been a target in the world for no apparent reason, just that I'm not liked. We have to understand that sometimes the Spirit within us will aggravate that which is in the world. It's hard when we experience these things to remain Christlike, though, isn't it?

I think that at this time of controversy we read in this portion of scripture we see a divide in the people, which is still present in the world today. What Jesus does here is remain steadfast. He points to the Father and that's something we can learn to do too. He doesn't take it personally. He understands where they are and what they believe but sticks to the truth.

My last question to ponder this week is:

Can you call to mind the hopelessness of someone who's walking without Jesus at the moment and begin to empathise with them?

The answer to this question may just enlighten you to circumstances that you can pray into on behalf of other people. If it does, why not use this as one of your 'Respond' steps this week and commit to praying specifically for that person and document the change you see.

Life Flow

WEEK 22

Read John 7:37-52

This week we continue to look at the divided opinions amongst the people regarding who Jesus was. I think it's fascinating to see all the different comments. I can certainly see some similarities to this day and age also, you only have to look at what's going on in any sort of political dispute to see how this must have looked. I love, though, how Jesus waits until the most important day of the festival to announce prophetically what will happen as people accept His living water: He was speaking about the Holy Spirit (see Isaiah 44:3, 55:1, 58:11, Ezekiel 47:1 and Revelation 22:1).

What I find most captivating about the portion of scripture, though, is the differences of opinion and the people who state those opinions. I think about what might be going on with them to draw them to the conclusion they have. Some said He was a prophet, some the Messiah, some couldn't comprehend what good or anointed figure could come from Galilee, some spoke of His descent from David's bloodline, some wanted Him arrested and others feared touching Him. I'm most struck by the opinion of those who have actually encountered Him. I touched on this a little last week; I talked about our difference in the world whilst we carry the Holy Spirit, but this week I want to look at what we do differently.

Looking at the return of the temple guards in this portion we can see that there's something different about them when they come back; they've seen something that has changed their perspective and it antagonises the Pharisees.

My first question for you today is:

Can you think of something you now do or an opinion you now have that's totally different to before you encountered Jesus?

I encountered Jesus as an adult. I wasn't bought up in a Christian home and I didn't have any influence around me at all growing up to create an environment for me to know Jesus. You might say it's easy for me to recall those experiences being so fresh in my mind. You might have grown up in a Christian family and were taught all about the goodness of God, therefore you would say it's harder to recall the times you've really had a life-changing revelation. If that's the case I beg to disagree with you. I have a friend who was brought up a Christian; she openly professes that it wasn't until a few years ago that she really encountered the life-changing flow of Jesus, she received the Holy Spirit and her life began to change dramatically. Just because we are brought up with a belief owned by parents doesn't mean that we have our own faith. The environment we bring our children up in influences their walk with Jesus and we should be constantly creating an environment that glorifies Him, but it's their heart for transformation and desire for relationship with Him that shapes their lives. The point I'm making here is that through the life flow of our relationship with Jesus we should be continually growing and receiving revelation on things we navigate during our lifetime. If we aren't there's something wrong.

How are you seeing the growth in your own walk with Jesus? What differences do you see today than six weeks ago?

After encountering Jesus, the temple guards came back with a different opinion than the one they went to challenge Jesus with. The Pharisees were appalled by this. Their response was to mock them and ask why, when their leaders weren't following Jesus, would they think that this was appropriate.

The fact is we are all leaders in our own right; we influence people all of the time. When we follow Jesus and commit to be a disciple it's our responsibility to lead people to Him by living according to His will for our lives. I'm a mum of three boys and I feel pressure to make sure I do this well. To walk with integrity and try to reveal Jesus to them daily is hard, especially with the added frustration of work, serving at church and meeting the expectations of everyone else around me. Some days I feel like a downright failure and am incredibly thankful for grace! Overall, though, I'd like to think that my boys see Jesus in me and understand what it is to live for Him.

The last dispute we read in this chapter is when Nicodemus comes to the defence of Jesus; little did the Pharisees know he, too, had spent time with Him. Nicodemus used his knowledge of the law to defend Jesus. I love how each and every time they persecute Him their own law bites them on the bottom! This portion of scripture is yet another example of the religious not knowing their scripture. If you look at the footnotes in The Passion Translation, it informs us that Jonah came from a village only three miles from Nazareth and it's also believed that Elijah, Nahum and Hosea also came from Galilee, not to mention Jesus' Galilean ministry was prophesied in Isaiah 9:1-2. This reminds me of the scripture in Proverbs 16:18 in The Message: 'First pride, then the crash – the bigger the ego, the harder the fall.' I have always found the more that I think I know only proceeds to teach me how much I don't actually know!

I think you will agree that in conclusion to today's devotion we can see that the people here who defended Jesus all had one thing in common, or should I say One thing. They had all spent time with Jesus and that resulted in them becoming more humble, softer in heart and open minded towards His presence. The only way to find true peace is to allow His flow of living water to run through our heart, allow His embrace to inform our opinions and let that water gush from us into all of the circumstances we face on a day-to-day basis. The final question I have for today is:

Are you allowing His river to flow in and then to flow out to those around you? What do you think those around you see?

Cast the First Stone

WEEK 23

Read John 8:1-11

It's easy, isn't it, to cast a stone of judgement when someone has done you wrong? In the last couple of weeks, we've talked about looking at other people's opinions with an empathetic heart and how we can shift our perspective. But what about when someone has done something to you that was deliberately wrong and hurtful?

In this week's Bible reading a woman and man are caught in the act of adultery. 'Caught in the act' gives me reason to believe that they were burst in upon by the religious leaders; they would have probably been naked, and the text tells us that the lady was dragged through the public area into the temple where Jesus was teaching. There would have been a lot of people listening to Jesus too. How awful! Now, the law was that both adulterers should be brought before the court, yet this isn't what happened; the man was left to get off scot-free! The Pharisee's had no regard at all for this woman, their only concern was to catch Jesus out. I'd like to use the text this week to look at how we deal with hurtful sin and what this story teaches us about dealing with it.

I come from a home that was broken. This all happened when I was 8 years old. I remember the day Dad came home to tell me he was leaving as clear as a bell; of course my recollection of that will be totally different to his and my mum's. As we've discussed we all see things differently and carry things that are informed by our own perspective, so what I am writing here is from my perspective which is not to cast blame or judgement on those I believed were responsible for hurting me. On 28th December 1989 I'd been to a Christmas party at our local social club with my mum. Dad wasn't there but he was waiting for us at home. My parents sat me down and Dad informed me that he was in love with someone else and he would not be living with us anymore. It cut to the core. I remember my mum's sadness and him leaving; she chased after the car as he pulled away. When she came back into the house, she asked how I felt. I said 'angry'. Then I think she asked me what I wanted to do with that anger. I chose to smash his favourite beer tankard across the patio in the garden. It made me feel better for a moment. Because I was a child and I had an innocent heart, my only concern at this time was that I liked the woman my dad was going to be with and it was an added bonus that she had a baby girl, the sister I'd always wanted! I had no idea how my conclusion of events would hurt my mum at that time. As time went by it was increasingly obvious that my mum was struggling to come to terms with this abandonment. There were people who would visit and one in particular even told me that it was now my responsibility to look after my mum; little did she know I would take these words quite literally for the rest of my life. My view of this situation for many years was that the hurt that was caused was deliberate. Some might say it was. My point is that whether it was or it wasn't, judgement and throwing stones doesn't help heal the pain.

In the first question to reflect on today I'd like to ask:

Is there a time in your life when you've been deliberately hurt by someone?

I talk about my broken family because it's an example of an action that can be seen as something deliberately done regardless of consequences. It had a huge impact on my life and it's something that I have applied the principles of this story in order to heal from it. It is in no way for people to read and cast judgement on those involved. If anything, I pray that people read this and have more understanding that the action is the sin to resent, not the people committing it.

In this story Jesus is protecting the one caught in the act of sin. He has the religious leaders think about their own sin by writing in the dust. It isn't documented as to what He wrote that day, but it did fulfil yet another prophecy that is found in Jeremiah 17:13: those who commit spiritual adultery against God will be written in the dust. All of the people there that day had sinned and were hypocrites. They had committed adultery against God and broken His heart by forsaking Him, yet they claimed to be closer to Him than any other!

In the suffering of my parents' break-up and carrying the weight of my mum's pain, I couldn't see the hurt in my dad, my stepmum or my stepsister. I didn't understand that there were reasons beyond my suffering that I was yet to or may never know. By the time I reached adolescence, I was bitter, angry and very resentful. All I could focus on was the hurt and the betrayal. I had no idea of the reasons, not that these reasons are excuses but they do help us to heal. Had I understood it a little bit better, I wouldn't have been so resentful. Due to the resentment, I became extremely rebellious and made some shocking life decisions which were all blamed on the hurt I was carrying, therefore sinning just as much as the initial sin!

Does this all sound familiar? Adam and Eve chose the wrong thing. God gave us free will and the whole Bible documents decisions and wrongdoing based on the pain and suffering induced on one another by one another!

In order to break free from this orphan spirit and the feeling of being abandoned and unwanted I needed a different perspective. The perspective of the One who created me. The One who died for me. I needed to understand that He created me and He created those that hurt me. He loved me and He loved them despite what they or I did. These circumstances and the pain cannot define us in order to live the life God wants for us.

My second question for you to reflect on today is:

Can you visualise God's love for the person you wrote about who hurt you?

As I began to experience God's love and understand my identity in Jesus, I began to see others too. I then began to feel His love for them and understand that it isn't the sinner we should hate, it's the sin. The Bible tells us, 'For we are not fighting against flesh-and-blood enemies, but against evil rulers and authorities of the unseen world, against mighty powers in this dark world, and against evil spirits in the heavenly places' (Ephesians 6:12 NLT). So, what if we take our eyes of what people are doing and have our eyes on who they are, just like Jesus did with this lady?

It wasn't easy to break free from the pain and suffering of the lies I'd been believing for the majority of my life but now I can honestly say I feel freedom like I've never felt before. I no longer cast stones and accuse those who I think are responsible for hurting me because I know that it isn't their fault. In fact I love them all the more for it! Sometimes things happen and I wander back to being hurt and offended, but each time I recognise that I recall the words Jesus spoke on the cross, 'Forgive them for they know not what they do.'

The last question I have for you today is:

Is there someone you need to forgive?

The way I generally identify the need to forgive someone is whenever I feel those old lies creep into my heart. Am I feeling rejected or left out? Do I resent something? Am I bitter or frustrated at something? Am I feeling inadequate? Am I judging someone based on their actions? If the answer is 'yes' to any of these questions I need to begin to understand why. Usually there will be a hurt from someone there, intentional or not, that needs to be dealt with. I found Bethel Sozo ministry tools to be particularly helpful in dealing with these issues. If you want to learn more about those tools, check out their website (www.bethelsozo.org.uk).

Light of the World

WEEK 24

Read John 8:12-30

Following the ordeal of the adulteress woman forgiven, the relentless nature of the religious leaders attacking Jesus continues. In the next portion of scripture we read the dialogue between them. Again, what strikes me here is the certainty of Jesus in who He is. I read somewhere that if we each knew without a shadow of a doubt who we were in Christ, and what we were called to do, we would step into that without fear and the world would be a very different place. But how easy is it to continually remind ourselves of that and push on without any fear?

The promise in verse 12 is that those of us who embrace His life-giving light will NEVER walk in darkness! So, what is it we are afraid of? I believe that God-planted desires lie in all of us, and those desires will form and shape our part of the world. We can actually change the world with the desires God gave us! How amazing is that?

Jesus tells the Pharisees in verse 14: 'Just because I am the one making these claims doesn't mean they're invalid. *For I absolutely know who I am*, where I've come from, and where I'm going. But you Pharisees have no idea about what I'm saying.'

He knows who He is, where He has come from and where He is going.

Because we carry Jesus within us, we too are light of the world. Our job is to embrace Him in order to shine as bright as we can amongst darkness. Church is a place where we all come together and shine, each playing a different part of His body. We edify the body, that's one another, and release each other to go out as individual beacons to shine in the darkness. Sounds simple, doesn't it? And it is, but only when we hold on to these three fundamental truths that Jesus knew about Himself.

Let's look at the first one. Jesus said, 'I absolutely know who I am.' That wasn't, 'Well, I know my name's Jesus' it was 'I know one hundred percent who I am.' Despite the abuse He was having to deal with He didn't waiver. Can we say the same for ourselves?

I see so many people today that struggle with who they are. We live in an age where people are struggling with so many areas of their identity it has become the norm to hide who we are and what we want to achieve. That's not the way God wants it. He plants the desires in our hearts from birth, He planned before the beginning of time our purpose. Can you imagine the pain He feels as we shy away from that? Life is a responsibility we are given; we can either sit back and let it pass us by or we can step up and say I'm going to achieve the purpose I was designed specifically for. But in order to do that we need to be really honest with who we are. We need to overcome our insecurities and be bold and courageous by seeking our identity through Jesus. We shine by embracing Him not embracing the world.

So, the first question for today is:

Who does God say you are?

The next thing that Jesus knows is where He came from. We, too, need to know where we came from. The first thing to hold on to is that you are a creation of God, formed for a purpose, planned before time, fearfully and wonderfully made. Once we got here the world then took hold and began to form and shape us through our experiences. Some of those things will be bad, some good. But irrespective, the Word tells us that God brings all things together for good. Those experiences play a part in forming the desires of our hearts. For example, I wrote last week about my parents' break-up and how I battled with abandonment because of that. Now one of the desires of my heart is to help those experiencing that pain to feel that they belong and are loved. Also, my life has changed so much through the power of the word that another desire is to study it, hence this devotional. Do I struggle with insecurity to get to this point? Yes! You wouldn't believe the battle I've had to get these words on paper. But knowing my identity, allowing God to sustain me and the desire to see things changed through it, far outweighs the fear and insecurities. By strengthening ourselves in God's truth we find that we can be as courageous as He instructs us to be.

So, the next question today is:

Where have you come from and what desire for change do you have?

The final things Jesus knows is where He is going. He knows He's going to be with the Father, as do we. But I also think He has a rigid plan here. He knows what He needs to do next, when and where. There's a quote by a gentleman called Les Brown that goes, 'The graveyard is the richest place on earth, because it is here that you will find all the hopes and dreams that were never fulfilled, the books that were never written, the songs that were never sung, the inventions that were never shared, the cures that were never discovered, all because someone was too afraid to take that first step, keep with the problem, or determined to carry out their dream.'

The sad fact is that we could go to be with Jesus without having fulfilled the purpose He gave to us. Without knowing where we are going, we will never achieve what we've been put here to achieve. Fear will always hold you back; it's our job to embrace our identity, purpose and run with endurance.

Where are you going? What is it you need to do next to achieve what your purpose is?

Embrace the Truth

WEEK 25

Read John 8:31-59

The last portion of chapter 8 is a lot to get my head around, I'm not sure if you will agree. I'm not a theologian and I like to read the Word to reflect on how I live my life. History and languages were never my strong point; in fact, I failed both subjects at school. However, I do grasp the freedom that is available to us as Jesus describes, unlike the Pharisees.

In verse 32 Jesus speaks of embracing the truth which sets us free. He's explaining that the bondage the people are in is related to religion. They weren't free because they were devoted to traditions set by man to strive for freedom. They embraced rules and regulations and created divisions for those not elite. Embracing the truth and pursuing a relationship with Jesus would be the only way to experience genuine freedom. The word 'truth' in this verse in Greek is 'reality'. Which means embracing the reality of Christ is to become free. It is only then that it's possible to feel the tangible love of God. That love has the ability to release us from captivity. This then drives us to discover His character more accurately along with His purpose for our lives. The day I encountered the tangible presence of the Holy Spirit was the day I knew I was committed to discovering all I could about the Father and the Son. I believe that this experience is one very different to confessing that you are a Christian. To encounter tangible love, we first need to surrender.

With this in mind the first question today is:

Is there anything that is holding you back from encountering the tangible love of God?

Jesus then goes on to talk to them about their father, whom they believe is Abraham, but Jesus is describing Satan, the one who is deceiving them into believing they are living in freedom whilst bound to religion and legalism. Satan is the father of lies and his job is to kill, steal and destroy. The fact of the matter is that when we partner with anything other than the truth we are partnering with Satan, and that's just what is going on here. The belief that they are set apart and closer to God than any other, the belief that they need to strive for the Father's love, the belief that anyone born with any ailment is subject to sin in their bloodline and to be ostracised from society are all lies that these people partner with. These lies are similar to ones that we might believe. We've talked previously about unforgiveness, resentment and self-loathing, but all these things are from Satan. In order to become free from them we need to continually renew our minds and replace these lies with the truth, which takes commitment. This commitment comes from the reality of Jesus in our lives.

My first day at church, I was given a little pocketbook of the Gospel of John. I'd come home from church on Sunday and sit down to read it. Line by line I'd read and find myself thinking, I have absolutely no idea what relation this book has to do with my life! Yet in church I'd find the preacher would speak directly into my heart. It was just really hard to read. I thought maybe it's the book. So, I asked my pastor for a proper Bible. She gave me a copy of the New Testament; it was the Abundant Life New Living Translation version. I felt like a grown up going home with it! But still I would read and have nothing to say for it. It took weeks of perseverance until one day I had something going on in my life and the Bible spoke directly into that situation! I was so excited at the revelation I missed (for a moment) that it was a rebuke to humble myself! Growing in spiritual maturity takes time and commitment, if we are determined to live for Jesus then we must commit to seeking Him wholeheartedly for our lives.

My next question for today is:

Is there something that stands out to you that God revealed through His word?

Freedom comes from embracing the truth; without it we will never know our identity or purpose. Jesus loves us all and wants us to be reconciled with God. He wanted it for the Pharisees too, but they were too blind and proud to receive it. He existed long before Abraham and Moses, who they were committed to following, but because they couldn't comprehend that, they were too stubborn to let go of their authority. Jesus was the One who they read about daily when they would read from the scriptures in the temples, He was the One who would set all the captives free, but they weren't having any of it.

Since the day of my first revelation I've not been able to put my Bible down. I read it most days (I'd like to say every day but that would be a lie!) and each time I receive new revelation and new freedom to consider. Are there things in my life that bog me down and knot me up? Yes. But time and time again I bring them to the feet of Jesus and learn how to handle them. I know it's hard and life is busy, but God is the timekeeper – if you allow Him the first fruits of your day, He will make sure the day ahead is one that you feel strengthened and protected in. You will be dressed from head to toe in armour ready to go to battle with any Goliath you face. You need only embrace the truth.

Where in your life do you need godly revelation?

Eyes Wide Open

WEEK 26

Read John 9:1-41

As we are reading a whole chapter of John this week, I'll keep the devotion short and sweet. This chapter is such a beautiful picture, jam packed with revelation, so I'm sure you will be blessed by it.

Jesus meets the blind man in this chapter, and we see Him mixing spit and clay to heal this man. This is the saliva that comes from the mouth of a man who is actually God Himself! Which is a wonderful picture representing the Word of God and how it has the ability to heal us, too. What I find really lovely in this story is that the spit that Jesus uses has also been the tool of the enemy throughout this blind man's life. Around this time in history, people believed that blindness was a curse and we see the disciples ask Jesus about that too. This man would be used to being rejected by people because of this, and was probably quite used to the sound of people spitting at him as they would walk by as he sat and begged, but this day was different!

Jesus came so that we might be free from fear, whatever that fear looks like He came to break the chains and He was using the very tool the enemy used to make this man feel rejected – His spit! This would be the last time that this poor man would ever associate spitting with a root of rejection.

I love how Jesus uses all things for our good; those fears imbedded in us He pulls them out gently and subtly, showing us how they can be used for good. We slowly but surely open our eyes to see a different perspective and we begin to understand how we've lived with that curse all of our lives, but actually we can take that pain and suffering and use it for the glory of Jesus. What a beautiful Saviour we serve!

This week's first question is:

What fear could Jesus be gently tugging at in you?

Jesus taught in the last chapter that He is the light of the world and here, as He turns darkness for this man to light, we see Him putting action to His words. The saliva and clay represent the water of the Word and fragility of man. By bonding the two together Jesus creates light for this man and light for the world to see. Through new eyes we begin to see the beauty of His love.

Jesus rubs the clay onto the blind man's eyes and then tells him to go and wash in the pool of Siloam which is when his sight is restored. In the same way, we are clay and when we are washed by the water of His Word our spiritual sight is restored.

Are there any areas of your life you feel blind?

In verse 38 the blind man throws himself at Jesus' feet and says, 'Lord, I believe in You!'

Let us think about that for a minute. He had been blind all of his life, he had never been able to read the scriptures, yet he had faith in Jesus. Again more evidence to suggest that the traditions and superficial knowledge of this day had a blinding effect on the religious leaders of the day. Many of them refused to believe and it's true today, too, that many have great knowledge of the Bible, but do they really have a deep-rooted belief?

What does your faith rely upon?

Walk Through the Gate

WEEK 27

Read John 10:1-21

Jesus is talking in this portion of scripture about a thief who comes to take away our identity and he's sneaky with it too. The parable gives the example of the gate, which is Jesus, allowing everyone in and out, by grace, to explore green pastures which is fullness of life. The gatekeeper is the Holy Spirit opening our hearts to allow the Good Shepherd, Father God in. We are the sheep and the thieves are, in this context, the Pharisees and false prophets who are, as previously discussed, controlled by the father of lies Satan.

The footnotes in The Passion Translation explain it's no coincidence that in the previous chapter Jesus had led the blindman out of his sheep pen to a new life of faith and relationship with the Good Shepherd. This is yet another beautiful picture of Jesus' actions aligning with what He preaches.

The false prophets and Pharisees that broke into the pen before Him came to steal, but what did they come to steal? I believe that they came to take the identities of those they saw as less than them. They wanted domination and power, they were rule makers and created rules that were impossible to keep. Creating a community of people who were bound up in what they proclaimed as sin, holding them firm in shame. Does that sound familiar? It does to me.

I talked previously about my poor life decisions as an adolescent and young adult; I was bound up in those choices and lived permanently in shame. Because of that shame I felt like I didn't deserve anything good to happen to me. I would isolate myself and make even worse decisions along with pushing people away. That's what the devil wants, he wants each and every one of us bound up in self-loathing, so much so that we either push everyone out or pull every other person around us down with us.

Jesus is describing the opposite in what He came to give us – life, freedom and satisfaction – so let me ask you:

On a scale of 1 to 10 how satisfied are you with your life at the moment?

Looking back, I think there have been times I could have scored zero in life satisfaction, but I was good at masking it. There was a void inside me that I could never fill; I tried with alcohol, drugs and meaningless relationships but never really felt satisfaction in my life until I met Jesus. I still believe that as a Christian I can also experience times in my life where I don't score a 10. When I experience a sense of discontentment, I know that there is something underlying and I need to deal with it. Jesus goes on to explain that the thief only has one thing in mind: to steal, slaughter and destroy. In other translations this is to steal, kill and destroy. With this in mind I think we can begin a process of uncovering the tactics Satan uses.

The first tactic might look like disappointment or frustration caused by theft. Theft of joy, peace, confidence or patience, a feeling you once had but now it's lost. I find that Galatians 5:22 is helpful. How do you score 1 to 10 on each fruit? If you score low on some it might be worth examining why that is. The devil comes to steal and if he can steal these fruits he can sneak into your heart and replace the truth with his lies.

The second tactic is death. Not physical death, but the expiration of a dream, a desire, a relationship, a job, a marriage, whatever it is you are feeling discontent with. Satan wants you to end anything that God desires for your life. So in the absence of love, joy, peace, patience, kindness, goodness, faithfulness, gentleness or self-control comes the presence of quarrelling, jealousy, bitterness, hostility, lustful pleasures, drunkenness, idolatry, whatever the devil needs to encourage you further away from the life God wants you to live. I might add here it's always very subtle.

The final tactic is destruction. By now you'll have lost your joy, given up on your relationships and feel the world is against you. But there's still hope, the Good Shepherd still calls to you. You know what you need to do but now, after ending the relationships or walking out of the job, you are filled with shame. The devil wants this to be the final destination. He fills our mind with lies. You can't possibly go back and apologise, so he adds more bitterness and hatred until you tip. Maybe you'll do something so shameful you can never show your face again. He wants total devastation and for you to never walk the path laid out for you again.

These stages don't always happen the way that I've described here; this is a short and very dramatic run down of how the devil sneaks in through open doors to take away the abundant life Christ died for us to have. They might happen very steadily over years. As I said, you may never go from 10 to 0 in a week. The devil is devious and that's why we have to continually guard our hearts and assess our emotions to understand where he might be sneaking in.

Can you identify any of the stages in your own life?

The good news is that we do not need to be fearful about this; the Good Shepherd knows whose hearts are His and He gave His life for those hearts overcoming the tactics of the thief. We are His sheep and have entered His fold. No matter what the devil tries to do we have a mighty God who can do more. The devil is under His feet, which means He is under our feet because we are in Christ and have all we need to fight his schemes. If you have identified any discontentment in your life today or that you are being the victim of theft, slaughter or destruction, you have the ability to give that back to Jesus, the One who gives life. You can lay down those lies at any time and ask the gatekeeper to allow you access through the gate to the Good Shepherd. Replace those lies with the truth and live again, a life of contentment and joy.

My last question for today is:

What would you like to lay down?

Still Small Voice

WEEK 28

Read John 10:22-38

Last week I talked about how the devil works in his schemes. This week I think you will see as you read through the portion of scripture how that's all worked out in the hearts of the Pharisees. They are so bound up in religion, pride and wanting to destroy Jesus that they have no idea of the truth; even though they read the scriptures daily they can't see that their Messiah is stood before them. They've been deceived by theft of the truth, their hearts slaughtered by their false religion and their future looks to be one of destruction.

Have you ever been in a situation where no matter how many times you repeat your account of events the person in front of you will not take your word for it? Maybe you've shared your faith with an unbeliever or tried to diffuse a battle between family members or friends. No matter what you do or say it's not going in. They don't want to believe the truth and the more you say, the more aggravated the person you're speaking to gets. I find in times like these it's easier to step aside.

I recall a time I was chatting with a group of friends; we were talking about watching our words and thoughts. I mentioned that we first have to let a rogue thought into our mind and entertain it before speaking out. One of my friends had been going through a really tough time and she took complete offence to what we were discussing. Because of what I had said she accused me of making her feel unworthy and condemned. I was mortified! Not only was it an innocent conversation and I hadn't pointed out anyone's sin, I wasn't qualified to do so. Despite her perception, I, too, have rogue thoughts and on occasions am known to say something I shouldn't! I did my best at the time to chat with her and help her understand that she's not condemned or a bad person. Later on that day I received a phone call. This lady was dealing with some things in her life and God was challenging her; as we discussed guarding our thoughts and words, she was convicted of some things that she had done and could change. They were hard for her to accept so she had used me as a punch bag. She apologised, and we prayed together and that was that.

After that phone call I didn't follow up about dealing with what it was the Holy Spirit was asking the lady to do. Why? Because it was clear to me at the time that no matter what I said I was making the situation worse. I knew that I needed to step aside and let the Holy Spirit do His work. It wasn't for me to fix. In today's 'Reflect' section I'd like us to think about any times in our lives we have struggled with these types of issues.

Is there someone that you've tried to share the truth with who has taken offence and seems to push you away as a result of it?

Thankfully, the lady I spoke about heard the soft whisper of the Holy Spirit, which is what Jesus is referring to in verse 27. She knew that there was something in her heart she needed to deal with and because of that she called and apologised to me. Jesus knows what we are feeling and, more to the point, has experienced it Himself. He promises us that by listening to that voice we will never be lost, and NO-ONE has the power to snatch us away. That's powerful stuff, isn't it? No matter what, we will never be lost, we need only listen to His voice. The problem with the Pharisees and those following them is that they were listening to the voice of those in power, not the still small voice of Jesus. They were fearful of those who shouted the loudest and, as we've learnt, Jesus didn't need to shout the loudest.

What does it mean to you to know that you can never be taken away from Jesus?

In verse 36, Jesus tells the people that are about to murder Him that He has been uniquely chosen by God to do the beautiful works His Father sent Him to do. Now let's think about that for a moment. If Christ is uniquely chosen by God and He dwells within us, then that means we, too, are uniquely chosen by God. How does that feel? To know that the creator of the heavens and the earth chose you specifically to do beautiful works on this earth. It makes me want to jump for joy. It gives me the motivation to write these words. It sets my heart on fire and pulls me through when times are tough. It allows me to dream and fix my eyes on all the wonderful things I can do with the gifts He's placed inside me. So, with this in mind, why don't we do a bit of dreaming.

If there were no restrictions at all what would you do with your life?

At the end of this chapter it tells us that many people became believers that day, because of the miracles they'd seen, the prophecies that came to be and the words that Jesus spoke. That's what happens when we submit ourselves to the will of God. The dream you just wrote about is something that God has exclusively chosen you for. He is going to use it for His glory, and it will win souls for His Kingdom. He knows that already; He's just waiting for you to get to it. So, what are you waiting for? Go do something today that brings you a step nearer to your God-given purpose.

Run the Risk

Read John 11:1-20

This is an amazing story about revival of life, but it was one with a great risk. At the beginning of this story we see the disciples feeling quite fearful about returning to Judea to save Lazarus, and Jesus doesn't seem to be in a hurry at all. The disciples were so pessimistic about returning and couldn't comprehend why Jesus would want to run the risk of losing His life to wake someone up! It makes me wonder about what risks I'm prepared to take to do the will of God in my life. Would I travel somewhere I knew I'd be in danger in order to win souls for Jesus? Would you?

There was a time in my life when I felt God calling me and my family away from a church we were in, to a church that was more local to our house. It was a relatively new church and we were very unsure about the move. We had to leave behind all that we knew to enter a new season of our lives, and with change, I think you will agree, comes uncertainty. Unlike the journey that Jesus and His disciples were about to take, it wasn't a move that threatened our lives. All the same, this passage got me thinking about how we deal with change and risk. Are we full of hope or full of fear?

The question to kick off today's devotional is:

Is there something God is asking you to do or change at the moment? If so, how does that feel?

I think that these verses teach us a lot about faith. Mary and Martha knew who would save their brother; as soon as they knew he was ill they called upon Jesus. It's something that we all need to do in times of uncertainty and some of us are better than others at this.

I have three boys; my youngest son has suffered since he was 9 months old with a chest condition. Asthma runs in my family which makes it likely that he has inherited that condition. Each time he's ill my first thought is to pray and ask God to heal him. There have been many times in the early hours I've been on my knees in his room begging God to move and open his airways so we don't have to spend time in hospital. I'd like this to be a testimony of miraculous healing, but it isn't. It always felt like God wasn't answering me. Just as we see here, Jesus didn't attend Lazarus and his sisters straight away, He waited. He waited because the plan was much greater than healing Lazarus from his sickness; the plan was to raise him from the dead.

God has a plan for my son. I have no idea what that plan is, and as much as I want him to not suffer with this chest condition, I have to have faith that God knows what's best for him. Please don't think here that I'm saying God is making him suffer. He isn't. Each time we go to hospital my son is treated and improves within hours, but what I'm saying is that in the suffering God has a plan. As I've previously said, I've met so many mothers on that hospital ward and had the opportunity to share my faith and pray with them. God is using me and my son to plant seeds in the hearts of these people in their hour of need also.

Have there been times in your life that you've prayed but feel God is taking His time or not answering in the way you would like?

The raising of Lazarus from the dead seemed to only be on the agenda of Jesus that day. The people around Him responded in many different ways. Thomas' response was almost sarcastic. He thought that by going back to Judea they were putting themselves at risk of death and he was filled with fear. When Jesus arrived at Mary and Martha's house, Mary decided to stay in the house; was that because she was upset with Him for taking His time? We don't know what exactly these people were feeling at the time, but we do know that this time gap was to allow Jesus to perform a miracle in front of the right people at the right time.

To have peace in chaotic circumstances is not something that comes naturally. But with God all things are possible. He wants us to walk with faith and not fear. So, this story is one that teaches us how we should respond in situations that seem hopeless. The Word tells us that God brings ALL things together for good and, no matter what, we need to stand upon that truth. When my son is ill now, I see those hospital visits as opportunities. They are times when I can bond with him, read to him, rest with him, pray with him and with those around us. He gets to make new friends and I do too. On one of our earlier visits to A&E I met and stayed in touch with a lady who had a very poorly baby. She also goes to church and was learning to rest in the peace of the Holy Spirit when her daughter was admitted to hospital.

What if we took a different perspective and chose to look for seeds of faith when we encounter trials? I think that's what Jesus meant when He said, *'Are there not twelve hours of daylight in every day? You can go through a day without the fear of stumbling when you walk in the One who gives light to the world. But you will stumble when the light is not in you, for you'll be walking in the dark'* (John 11:9).

Is there a situation you face at the moment that you could possibly reframe to Jesus' way of thinking?

Moved with Compassion

WEEK 30

Read John 11:21-39

Isn't it beautiful to read here about the compassion that Jesus had for His friends? He knew that He would raise Lazarus from the dead but was deeply moved to see the pain of Mary and Martha mourning. I don't know about you, but I don't often think about how moved Jesus is when I am suffering, but the truth is, He is. He hurts when we hurt. He knows the pain we feel, and He, too, has felt that pain. When I'm hurting and suffering, when I cry out to Him, it helps to remind myself that He hurts for me.

There have been so many times in my life I've been disappointed or rejected and I've called out to God for help. There have also been many times that I've struggled with things and not called out to God. I've tried to muster on in my own strength but become disgruntled, bitter and resentful. The reason we become that way is that we weren't created to do this alone. We were created to live a full life in Christ, not on our own.

One particular time that I struggled was at the death of a dream. Not a person but something that I grieved all the same. I'd not been chosen for a job that I'd gone for and it hurt. It hurt all the more, I think, because I was told they felt it was of God to not allow me to go into that role. I can't begin to tell you how much I cried. I began by shouting at God, asking Him why He had rejected me. As I began to soften and became less angry, I asked Him to help me to see why the other person had been chosen. As I spent more and more time seeking Him over this rejection, I began to see that I wasn't ready for the role I had gone for. My perception began to change, and I started to see doors open doing things that I loved to do. Those things didn't include the administration of the role I'd gone for. It was ironic, really, because I don't like to do administrative tasks! I'm much more of a hands-on person. The reality was that this job was definitely not for me. If I'd allowed the rejection to motivate my actions in this season, I could have been robbed of the things I love to do and the role that God wanted me in. Instead I chose to cry out to Him and have Him heal my heart over the situation.

Is there a circumstance that you can recall where Jesus has wept or may have wept with you?

If you take a look in the footnotes to The Passion Translation you will see a note on verse 25: Jesus is explaining to Martha that He is 'the Resurrection' and 'Life Eternal'. Which means in Him, as we cling to Him in faith we, too, are resurrected. We enter into a life that is superior and cannot be defeated. Resurrection is the power to conquer all; life is merely the power to exist. The only way to this life is through Jesus. We must learn to live in Him at all times and His ability to conquer all things. That is having faith that no matter what we face He will conquer it for His glory and our eternal life. It's yet another perspective that we need to carry when we navigate the day to day. The notes then point us to look at Philippians 3:10 which says:

And I continually long to know the wonders of Jesus more fully and to experience the overflowing power of his resurrection working in me. I will be one with him in his sufferings and I will be one with him in his death.

What do you think it means to know the wonders of Jesus more fully?

I really love these verses in John 11. I think we really see a picture of Jesus' heart for those He loves and who love Him too. There's something really special about the relationship here that we can learn about our relationship with Him. His heart is for us and to be with us. In verse 28 Martha runs to her sister and whispers in her ear that Jesus is calling her by name. Immediately Mary runs to Him and that, too, is what we should be doing. He's calling us by name, He wants us to run with open arms towards Him. He wants to hold us tightly and whisper over us life-giving truth that will set us free. But we have to want that. We were created to worship Him, but we can't worship someone we don't know that well. He wants us to be intimate with Him and bring to Him all of our hearts; not just the bits we are OK with handing over to Him but the mucky bits too. The feelings and emotions we don't want anyone to know about, He wants those too. He knows that they are there, we can't hide. He just wants us to want to freely give these insecurities over to Him in exchange for some life-giving truth. He wants you to experience overcoming, empowering, mind-shifting resurrection life!

What does your resurrection life look like?

Unbound

WEEK 31

Read John 11:40-57

The last part of chapter 11 is all about Lazarus. Well it's not, it's all about the life-giving love of God! But in the context of the devotional I want to look at what happens as Lazarus is brought back to life and how that might look on our journey of discipleship. For the last couple of weeks we've looked at how we live life with Jesus and what that changes for us, how that change can feel risky, how Jesus hurts for us and how our thinking can begin to change as we understand that. So, this week is all about breaking free.

Lazarus was raised from the grave and the description of him coming out of the tomb is that he hobbled out in his grave clothes. What a sight that must have been! As he comes out of the tomb Jesus instructs the people around him to help Lazarus out of his grave clothes. In that day it was custom to wrap the body tightly in white cotton cloths from head to toe. So he would have kind of hopped out of the tomb, I think. I love that Jesus asked the people around, though, to help him become unbound.

To me this is a picture of salvation. The day that we meet with Jesus and invite Him to live within our hearts we are given new life. It's the rebirth that Jesus talks to Nicodemus about back in John 3. The Holy Spirit enters our heart and makes His dwelling place within us. We are a new creation, raised from the dead just as Lazarus is here. Even though we are a new creation there may be some things that we take from our old life into our new, or things that happen as we navigate through the world that might bind us up in wrong thinking. Just as Jesus instructed the people to help Lazarus out of His grave clothes, we are instructed to help those around us too.

The grave clothes to me represent anything that is holding us back from the abundant life we talked about when we looked at John 10:10. Jesus came so that we might have a life of fullness. An abundance of life with eternity in mind as we journey through our trials. The problem is that sometimes things happen to hold us back from that. One of the things that I struggled with is critical thinking. I've mentioned before that one of the issues I've had to deal with is fear of rejection. When I feel rejected, I can experience a mindset that consistently criticises everything! It's to do with pride too. I think that as I became more insecure, I'd guarded myself with pride and think I knew better than everyone around me. If I knew better, I'd never have to ask for help, then I wouldn't be rejected. Critical thinking, fear of rejection and insecurity became my grave clothes and had me hopping around restricted and confined to relying on myself. But that's not what God wants for us. Being on your own mission, too frightened to trust the people around you, only gives way for isolation and that's just where the devil wants us. Alone.

Are there any grave clothes that are keeping you bound?

One of the biggest tools the enemy uses to keep us bound up is offence and that generally comes from fear of rejection or insecurity in us. When we become offended the natural thing to do is retreat and cut ourselves off. That's not what God wants for us, He does not want us to be alone. He gave us one another to be a community. He told Adam and Eve to be fruitful and multiply in the beginning, His intention was never for us to be a family of one. James 5:16 says:

Confess and acknowledge how you have offended one another and then pray for one another to be instantly healed, for tremendous power is released through the passionate, heartfelt prayer of a godly believer!

How can we do this with one another if we are cut off? Church is the most irritating place in the world at times, but it's meant to be! Families are meant to get irritated with one another. You can't share a life together without becoming a little annoyed at one another at times.

When I first got together with my now husband one of the things that irritated me the most about him was his constant questioning while we were watching a film. He still does it now, and we are married. I learnt to live with it. I also learnt to tell him that it irritated me and guess what? I still love him, and he still loves me despite that irritation. I'm sure if I allowed him to write some things here, he would tell you some things I do that irritate him, like get my hair everywhere – it has even been known to land in his cup of tea! The point I'm making here is that the community of God, His church, is a family and families are dysfunctional – why should it be any different in God's family?

Who has God placed around you to help you remove the grave clothes?

We have each other because Jesus wants His body connected and united to bring glory to His Father, just as He did in this chapter. We might not be called to physically raise people from the dead, but we are all called to help remove one another's grave clothes. Whatever is binding His family up He wants it removed and you are the one to help remove those binds. So, the last thing to ponder today is:

Who can you help to remove their grave clothes?

Extravagant Worship

WEEK 32

Read John 12:1-19

This chapter is all about a lady who pours everything she has on to Jesus in her worship to Him. The perfume that she anoints His feet with is most likely an inheritance and the most expensive thing that she owns. As I studied this chapter it got me thinking about my own worship to Jesus. Do I pour out all I have to Him as I worship Him? We all have different spiritual pathways in the way that we connect with the Father, the Son and the Holy Spirit but no matter how we worship Him I know He wants all of us as we do it. As I pondered my worship style, I thought about how sometimes I can become distracted and start worrying about what is going on around me.

I recently went to a conference where we were encouraged to worship with complete abandon. I was in awe at what was happening in that room as we praised God. There were all sorts of things going on: I saw people jumping around, flag dancing, painting, marching, laughing uncontrollably, laying on the floor completely away with the Holy Spirit – it was amazing to be a part of it. I felt completely free to do whatever I pleased in awe of God. It got me thinking about what it looks like in church on a Sunday; it's far from that event. Although I do think there's a time and a place for spirit-filled worship and we do sometimes see free flow worship on Sunday mornings, but I do find I'm more distracted on a Sunday in terms of what needs doing, who's watching, what my kids are up to and many other things that run through my mind after rushing to get to church. BUT the times that I do have head space to worship in complete awe things shift in my heart and I feel fully alive.

How do you feel after giving your all to worshipping Jesus?

The disciples thought that this woman was stark bonkers and Judas, the betrayer, was particularly annoyed at the waste of something that was worth so much. Which I think says a lot for our worship. It's worth a lot to Jesus. It means a lot. It determines where your heart is. If you are half-hearted in worship, it means that something isn't quite right. Mary was pouring everything she had on to Him in this moment because she knew that He would pay the ultimate cost. He was life, He deserved everything she had. She had a relationship with Him that had grown, she had learnt from Him and knew that He would give it all just for her.

The thing is, when we give our all to Him there is always someone like Judas who is going to question what an earth we are doing. I get it all the time; I'm sure there are many times I have conversations with people about my relationship with Jesus and they think I'm crackers. There may be people who read this book and think I'm talking utter rubbish, and that's OK. It's OK because I know where my heart is and so does Jesus. This is me pouring out my alabaster jar for Jesus and I'm not worried about the cost because I love the One who died for me. I love what He's done in my life and I want to tell people about it. I want people to experience His love in the tangible and beautiful way that I have. So what if some people think it's nonsense. Some won't and they will be the ones who will remember what it is to pour out their worship to Jesus no matter what the cost. Those who take the time to read this devotional will realise I'm just a bog-standard mum of three who loves Jesus and if I can write, so can they. We each have a story inside us that Jesus created so why not share it. If I can, you can too! It might not be a book you want to write, but whatever that costly act of worship is I want to encourage you to break that alabaster jar and take a step closer to it today.

What would it mean for you to break your alabaster jar?

Following Mary's act of worship, we see Jesus travel into Jerusalem and there were swarms of people there following His miracle of raising Lazarus from the dead. They wanted to see Jesus and Lazarus with their own eyes. The people were in awe, laying palm leaves on the floor, praising Him and shouting 'Hosanna', which means 'Lord save us'. All of which was prophesied many years before. The Pharisees knew that this would be uncontrollable. The more people gathered, the more people heard of the miracles and the more people believed. This is how it works, isn't it?

We see Lazarus raised from the dead, which is a picture of us being awakened by a call from Jesus; the grave clothes are removed with the help of the church community you are called into, and we become free to live the life God created us to. We then tell others and the cycle continues. Which is why I continue to encourage you that your story and your life is important, it's all part of your calling to serve Jesus; people want to hear it and people will be set free by hearing it. It's all on you whether or not you are prepared to break away from the fear of rejection in order to tell it.

Who can you begin to share your story with today?

They Will See Him Through You

WEEK 33

Read John 12:20-33

In this week's portion of scripture we see some Greek men go to see Philip and they ask him to take them to see Jesus. Jesus' response is a bit of a strange one, to be honest, and as I read it, I was a little baffled and had to look into it more before I understood what it meant. Then, when I understood it, I was bowled over. That's what I love about studying God's Word: there are always so many layers to it, I don't think I could ever become bored of it. Jesus says in verses 23-24:

Now is the time for the Son of Man to be glorified. Let me make this clear: A single grain of wheat will never be more than a single grain of wheat unless it drops into the ground and dies. Because then it sprouts and produces a great harvest of wheat – all because one grain died.

Basically, what Jesus is saying here is that the single grain of wheat is Him and when He dies, He will drop into the ground and there will be a great harvest of seeds, which is Philip and Andrew and, guess who else . . . Us! He is explaining to Philip and Andrew that the Greek men will see Jesus through them.

So, He is also explaining that as we follow Him and experience the dying and birthing of our new life, the people we encounter will also see Him. How amazing is that?!

When I think about all the people I encounter on a daily basis, I wonder if they can actually see Jesus at work in me. I know that at times that can be hard to believe, especially when we are stretched and strained by life's trials, but the fact remains it's the truth. If we commit to following Him then people we meet will see Him through us.

How does it make you feel to know that people will see Jesus at work in you?

So, what does it look like to really follow Jesus? In verses 25-26 Jesus continues:

The person who loves his life and pampers himself will miss true life! But the one who detaches his life from this world and abandons himself to me, will find true life and enjoy it forever! If you want to be my disciple, follow me and you will go where I am going. And if you truly follow me as my disciple, the Father will shower his favour upon your life.

According to the footnotes in The Passion Translation, 'follow me and you will go where I am going' can be translated in Greek text to, 'If anyone ministers to me (materially provides for me), where I am, my minister will be there too.' Meaning that a life of full surrender to God will make us a grain of wheat that multiples into a harvest. With this in mind I'd like to think about what that looks like, full surrender to God. So, let us ponder that in the 'Reflect' section for this week:

How do we live in complete surrender to God?

154

The next thing to happen was that God spoke! The actual audible voice of God was heard. The text says that it startled the crowd although there were divided opinions over what it was: some thought it was thunder, some said an angel spoke to Jesus. I have many conversations with people about what I feel God is saying in our lives. Some find this easy to decipher, others don't. Some say that they've never heard God speak to them, yet they believe in Jesus. I think that this all depends on where we are in our relationship with Him and how open we are to Him. It all goes back to surrender and the desire for His will in our lives, I think. If we have freewill then we need to make the choice of what level of surrender we are going to give to God. He wants us to give it all to Him, but He won't force us to do that.

Jesus said in verse 26 that if we truly follow Him as His disciple then God will shower His favour on our lives. I don't think this is the sort of bargain I have with my kids to eat their greens though. His favour on our lives may not look like the life we imagine; it's all part and parcel of trusting in Him. I heard this analogy in a sermon once that I thought was quite useful. When we are going off on a journey we pack up the car with our stuff and the kids sit in the back; they don't ask which way we are going or give us scenarios of occurrences and ask for us to explain how we might navigate them, they just sit and wait for us to get to the destination, with a few 'are we there yet' and 'I need a loo break' on the way. That's what we are to do with God. Trust in the journey that He will get us to the destination. That's complete surrender.

When we surrender, people see Jesus in us. When we follow Him with complete abandon there is something different about us to the world, but to do that requires trust. Is there something that you are trusting God for at the moment? Maybe there's something you've lost hope in. Maybe you've jumped into the driver's seat and have taken over. I don't know where you are in your walk but the last question for today is:

Is there something you need to surrender back to God?

Rising Above Rejection

WEEK 34

Read John 12:34-50

I've talked that much about it that I thought, hey, why not do a week's devotion on the subject! You all know by now one of the biggest fears I've struggled with is the fear of rejection. I am constantly battling with thoughts about what people think of me. I think we all do to a certain extent. People get the impression I'm confident and outspoken but that's a mask. Inside I'm quivering, wondering what people think of me and how they might respond, my childlike spirit desperate for a pat on the head and a nod of approval. This portion of scripture shows us yet another example of the rejection Jesus had to face. Now, He performed some mighty miracles, and if He gets rejected its inevitable that we will too.

Verse 40 takes us back to Isaiah's prophecy:

God has blinded their eyes and hardened their hearts to the truth. So with their eyes and hearts closed they cannot understand the truth nor turn to me so that I could instantly cleanse and heal them.

Sometimes, no matter how much people see Jesus at work in your life, the truth is they are still going to reject you because their eyes are blinded to His love. We are responsible for planting seeds although we may never see the harvest, but as long as we are planting, we are being obedient. We need to learn to deal with rejection and not allow it to affect our journey with Jesus or root lies into our hearts and discourage us.

My first question this week is:

How, when we are witnessing to people, can we learn to not take rejection personally?

My husband and I came to know Jesus as adults. Neither of us have family members who are Christians and, if I'm honest, still after all these years I don't think that they understand it's a relationship not religion. Last week I saw an interview with a celebrity from a programme I used to watch as a child, *Gladiators*. It was Ace (not the interview, the person). His screen name was Ace the Gladiator. He shared his faith on television. Not only that, he corrected them when they asked him how he found 'religion'. Religion is dutiful, people in religion are bound to it. Relationship is choice. Friends from our past also don't understand how we can be 'religious' either, after all our years of rule breaking and not conforming. But what they don't understand is that we have found a relationship in Jesus, and that relationship has shown us the character of our creator, our almighty Father. It's given us insight into our life purpose and why we exist. We are hardwired for that connection and the reason that people spend their whole lifetime searching is that they are blinded to the freedom that they can find in a relationship in Christ. God's heart is for everyone to know Him; we don't know when that will be but because of our bond with His son we have hope in that and faith that it will happen. This is the reason that we will go on witnessing despite the rejection we face or the opposition we come across.

We can't allow fear of rejection to distract us from those who God is calling. For each conversation I've had with someone that's fallen flat, I've had two that have been fruitful. I think this is what Jesus referred to in the portion we read last week, when He said that His true disciples will be showered with God's favour. We need to stay encouraged and strengthened as we walk. So how do we do that?

What are your main sources of encouragement?

I love to read but sometimes when I'm feeling dejected and down I find it difficult to concentrate. My favourite way to lift my spirit is to put on worship really loud and sing at the top of my voice! I'm certainly not a singer, but it's something that can take me from down in the dumps to high on life in minutes. It's a habit that I've formed over the years. Whenever I feel my heart becoming unsettled, I know it's time to take action. If we recognise the approach of discontentment, it's much easier to do something about it before it takes shape and affects our character or relationships.

The reason I'm explaining how I encourage myself is because as we read verses 42 and 43, we see that the Jewish leaders also feared rejection. The verses explain that there were many Jewish leaders who believed in Jesus, but they kept it a secret because they didn't want to be ostracised by the Jewish assembly. In order to keep fear at bay we need to be so full of the Spirit that our very presence radiates Jesus. By encouraging ourselves in the Lord we will not have space for fear of rejection. Our hearts will be so full in Him that we walk with Him and reflect His glory without thinking about it. In 1 John 4:18 we are told that perfect love casts out all fear, and it does, but it's our responsibility to unravel that gift from Jesus. The Jewish leaders loved the glory they got from men and not the glory they got from God because they'd spent so long keeping their belief a secret, they hadn't come to know Jesus at all. It's not good to be lukewarm. We cannot expect to live a life on purpose whilst keeping our faith a secret. We must press into Jesus and get to know our heavenly Father in order to understand what He wants for us.

On a scale of 1 to 10 how close do you feel to the Godhead – Father, Son and Holy Spirit?

Lesser Servant

WEEK 35

Read John 13:1-38

As we move on to John chapter 13, we draw closer to the death of Jesus on the cross. I actually went on to write 'the end of Jesus' ministry' here, but we know that is not the case; His ministry goes on. I then tried to say 'the end of Jesus' life' but again this is not the case; He is very much alive, and His ministry lives on, that's the true legacy!

The word 'minister' or 'ministry' derives from the word 'minus', which means 'lesser', which in this case would be described as 'a lesser servant of God': we are each a minister for God ordained by the greatest commandment, which we will see later today in the chapter we are studying. In this chapter we see Jesus serving His disciples.

The things we've witnessed throughout this book are always described as 'signs' by John and the reason he calls them signs is because they always point to something deeper. A fire exit sign points to a door; it's a sign to say there's something else here that will help you. That's why when we look at the Word of God it never grows old, there's always more. In verse 5 we see Jesus remove the disciples' sandals to wash their feet; this is a sign with a deeper meaning, according to the footnotes in The Passion Translation. Jesus is granting them a new inheritance. In Hebrew culture the sandal is often used in a covenant of inheritance, so this sign is that every defilement would be removed so that they could place the sole of their feet upon the new covenant inheritance, wherever their feet may fall.

I will give you every place where you set your foot, as I promised Moses. (Joshua 1:3 NIV)

This is also comparable to the moment Moses was ordained by God into his ministry. God told Moses to remove his sandals (Exodus 3:5); he was about to receive a new inheritance – the holiness of God and the authority that came with it. Considering this we see the ordination of God's servants; we, too, are ordained as His servants.

Is Jesus asking to wash your feet to allow you the inheritance of the holiness of God and authority that comes with it in order to 'minister' to those standing around you?

Think back to that day: there had never been a man of such authority perform such an act of service – no nobleman, teacher or king had ever loved his servants as Jesus did! Again, we see a glimpse of His legacy and He instructs them in verse 17 to put into practice what He has done. So here we see an instruction for our lives but, also, He reveals what will happen when we follow the instruction!

Have you ever performed an act of kindness or service that makes you feel warm inside?

I went on a girls' weekend away once. We went out to dinner at a nice restaurant and had one of the best three-course meals I've ever enjoyed. One of the girls couldn't finish her food. Before we went into the restaurant we'd seen a homeless man sitting outside; she decided to get the food put into a take-out bag and give it him – he was so grateful. When she came back, she went on to tell us that this is something she does regularly. She loved the feeling once she's given away a blessing – she wasn't a Christian. The point I'm trying to make is that it's ingrained in us to want to bless one another. We are made in His image, whether we know it or not we were created to love one another. The difference with us is that we have a relationship with Jesus and do it for Him and with Him, which gives us purpose. Giving without purpose only winds up in pride. We give the glory back to Him.

Despite knowing that Judas would betray Him Jesus washed his feet! He treated him no differently to the rest of them; Judas was just as much part of the plan as the rest of them! We see in verse 21 that He was moved deeply by the potential of His betrayal. There's a lesson here.

Is there a Judas in your life who's trying desperately to pull you down? If so, how could you get down on your knees and wash their feet?

Now, I'm not saying here that you go to them and physically do something – there may be circumstances that will not enable you to do that – but you can pray for them, you can stand in the gap and ask God to go to work on their behalf, you can ask for wisdom and knowledge surrounding that circumstance and you can ask God to help reframe your thinking to help you to see this from another angle.

We know that we are given the strength to do this because it was documented here in verse 26. In the day of the text, it was a cultural act of cherished friendship and intimacy to hand over a choice piece of food to a friend. So, knowing that Judas would betray Him Jesus still chose love. When receiving that gift, Satan entered Judas' heart, and in life sometimes we continue to have people who walk all over us, but Jesus shows us how to respond. Because God is our protection, we need not defend ourselves.

In verse 34 Jesus reiterates the acts of love He's just performed. Obviously the disciples at the time don't yet know that He's shown love to the very man who betrayed Him but we do; we see what we are instructed to do and we see the blessing we are promised as a result.

When Peter informs Jesus that he would give himself as a sacrifice in place of Him we see his resistance to see his weakness. We're all a bit like that, aren't we? Until the time comes, we are confident in our fleshly pride that we can do something, then in the moment we realise we don't have the strength in ourselves to follow through.

It's easy for me to sit here and write these words, to decipher and break down the text and explain the meaning to our life, but how easy is it for me to follow through, to love my enemy so much I find strength to pray for them, without bad mouthing them, without replicating their behaviour towards me? I can only do what is asked of me in the strength of the One who gave His life for me. I need to remind myself each day that I can only do this in Him; I must continually give up these woes and worries and allow Jesus to renew my mind.

What are you taking on in your own strength now that you know Jesus wants you to let go of it?

In Your Defence

WEEK 36

Read John 14:1-31

We are looking this week at how Jesus comforted His disciples. This chapter is all about the Comforter, the Holy Spirit and Jesus teaches them and us how He plays a part in our lives. Verses 1-4 tell us that we aren't to worry or surrender to our fear. The Aramaic here can be translated 'let not your heart flutter'.

Have you ever had that feeling of anxiety when you are fearful of something, where your stomach turns, and you feel a sickness rise to your throat? Here Jesus tells us how to overcome that very feeling. He says to the disciples that because they believed in God they are now asked to trust and believe in Jesus too; that instruction's also to us. This is our promise: we have a place of rest prepared for us beyond this world, so fear not, this is not it, those fears and worries we have in the world don't matter. No matter what trouble we face, illness we suffer, hurt or pain we go through, that is not the end, that's not the definition for our life; the definition is that we will go to the place Jesus has lovingly prepared for us!

Jesus mentions His Father's house in John 2:16, His temple on earth, His dwelling place, so Jesus isn't just talking about heaven when He talks of His Father's house. We know, too, that one of the dwelling places of God is a tabernacle; we also know that we are now living tabernacles carrying the very presence of

God, so we are one of His many dwelling places here on earth. Whilst Jesus is preparing a place for us, He is also preparing our place for God!

Don't you realise that together you have become God's inner sanctuary and that the Spirit of God makes his permanent home in you? (1 Corinthians 3:16)

This entire building is under construction and is continually growing under his supervision until it rises up completed as the holy temple of the Lord himself. This means that God is transforming each one of you into the Holy of Holies, his dwelling place, through the power of the Holy Spirit living in you! (Ephesians 2:21-22)

But Christ is more than a Servant, he was faithful as the Son in charge of God's house. And now we are part of his house if we continue courageously to hold firmly to our bold confidence and our victorious hope. (Hebrews 3:6)

How does it make you feel to know that you are part of God's Kingdom on earth?

Verse 15 talks of our love for Christ; this is a love that is demonstrated by obedience to do all He instructs us to. He doesn't want us to feel guilty of our sin, to feel unworthy. If we look at the footnotes in The Passion Translation for verse 16, we see that the word 'another' is interpreted 'allos' in Greek; it means 'another of the same kind'. Jesus is the Saviour from the guilt of sin, the Holy Spirit is the Saviour who saves us from the power of sin by living through us in fullness.

An example of that would be Jesus asking us to forgive our enemies. Let's say we are offended by someone and think that their actions towards us are a personal attack when in fact that person knows no different; all the same we are offended. Jesus tells us quite plainly to forgive them, but how can we?

We end up all stressed out, angry and really not wanting to be in a room with that person, but then there's a double edge to this because we know Jesus wants us to forgive them. When we think about it we end up feeling guilty, going over and over it in our minds until we feel condemnation, a lack of worth and we begin to wonder how 'Christian' we actually are!

The Holy Spirit offers us another way. When we feel this way, *if* we submit these feelings to Him, He will allow us to see things from another perspective. If we are humble enough to say that we know we are wrong for holding on to contempt for this person and give the Holy Spirit permission to do His thing, we will begin to see things that weren't visible before.

The footnotes to The Passion Translation also reveal in verse 16 the word 'saviour' is translated in Greek as *'paráklētos'*; it's a technical word that can be translated as 'defence attorney'. It means 'one called to stand next to you as a helper'.

So here we see God will give us another of the same kind of Saviour once Jesus has gone to stand to our defence, to help us and always stand with us – always!

Imagine a defence lawyer and how they go to work on their client's behalf; in short, they find things out about the prosecution case in order to confuse their evidence to convince the jury that their client has been wronged. The Holy Spirit will go on our behalf!

I can't tell you the amount of times I've been in a situation whereby someone or something made me out to be in the wrong; if I'd of gone to battle in my own strength on these occasions I would only have made things worse – our emotions get in the way and we do and say things that don't help. If we choose to instruct our defence lawyer *He* will go on our behalf, He will bring all things together for good!

Where in your life can you let go of control and allow the Holy Spirit to take over?

A wonderful explanation of the Holy Spirit is written by Brian Simmons using the Aramaic in his Bible translation The Passion:

> *Keep in mind that the Holy Spirit is the Spirit of Christ, our Saviour. The Aramaic word is* paraqleta, *which is taken from two root words: (1)* praq, *'to end, finish, or to save,' and (2)* lyta, *which means 'the curse'. What a beautiful word picture, the Holy Spirit comes to end the work of the curse (of sin) in our lives and to save us from its every effect!* Paraqleta *means 'a redeemer who ends the curse'. (See* Strong's Concordance, *Gr. 6561 and 6562; A Compendious Syriac Dictionary, p. 237; and Oraham's Dictionary, p. 250.)*

So, the Holy Spirit comes to end the work of the curse of sin in our lives and save us from its very effect! Guilt is from the enemy. Don't allow Satan to rob you of this wonderful gift we've been given; accept that there is something we can do about how we are feeling and give it to the Holy Spirit, allow Him to do a work in your heart about the things you are holding on to, cry out to Him. I can promise you that it will be the most liberating and freeing thing you have ever done in your life!

The Holy Spirit is our guide for life, our lifelong navigation system, He teaches us, comforts us, and defends us. He is fighting for us and ensuring that we live in the perfect peace Jesus describes in this portion of scripture. God has not given us a spirit of cowardly fear and these guilty lies keep us bound up in fear. In verse 27 Jesus uses the words that were spoken from the mouth of Moses before he died to Joshua as he was commissioned to take the Israelites to the promised land:

The Lord himself goes before you and will be with you; he will never leave you nor forsake you. Do not be afraid; do not be discouraged. (Deuteronomy 31:8 NIV)

Keep this Book of the Law always on your lips; meditate on it day and night, so that you may be careful to do everything written in it. Then you will be prosperous and successful. Have I not commanded you? Be strong and courageous. Do not be afraid; do not be discouraged, for the Lord your God will be with you wherever you go.' (Joshua 1:8-9 NIV)

Joshua said to them, 'Do not be afraid; do not be discouraged. Be strong and courageous. This is what the Lord will do to all the enemies you are going to fight.' (Joshua 10:25 NIV)

In verse 30 Jesus said, *'I won't speak with you much longer, for the ruler of this dark world is coming. But he has no power over me, for he has nothing to use against me.'* We are overcomers and the devil has no power over us. The words here aren't just words to the disciples, Joshua and the Israelites, they are for us too; these are our promises and instructions from God. He has put within us a courage that cannot be shaken, but it's our job to activate it.

How can you remind yourself daily of the courage you are given from God?

Don't Topple Over

WEEK 37

Read John 15:1-27

Jesus takes to Himself every single fruitless branch attached to us. He lifts them up off the ground and tends to them delicately, snipping away at each fruitless bit in order to benefit the good parts to flourish. Even though we each fall short we are loved beyond measure! No matter what we face Jesus says to us, 'Do not fear, for I am with you.'

What fruit are we trying to bear?

Galatians 5:22-23 lists nine fruits that we have in the Holy Spirit: love, joy, peace, patience, kindness, goodness, faithfulness, gentleness and self-control. If we find anything in our hearts that doesn't correlate with these fruits Jesus will prune away until they are defined in our lives. The Greek word for pruning is 'kathairo' which can also mean 'cleansing'; we are being cleansed from the inside out. Those deep-rooted issues that hold us back are the ones that Jesus will gently prune over time as we continue to press into Him.

As we already know, though, the devil comes to steal, kill and destroy. So, there are many times that we find ourselves bound up in confusion normally stemming from being attached to something other than Jesus. Being connected to the vine means to hold on to the truth; reminding ourselves continually of His love for us. The promise that He gives to us in the chapter is that, should we allow Him, He will create a fully flourished, blossoming, rooted firm, unshakeable, fruit-FULL, creation in us.

When we allow lies to creep in, we begin to wither; the more we partner with those lies, the less we drink from the goodness of His Word and we become dehydrated and wither some more. Before long we become so dry that we begin to perish, losing sight of the fullness of life we once had. The good news is that should we go back to the well, should we cry out to the vine, we will once again be filled, nourished and raised back to life.

One day, while my family and I were out exploring some woodland, we found a big old oak tree lying down across the ground. It had literally just unearthed itself and it lay across the ground with its roots on show. From what I could see, the roots beneath the tree were small, much smaller than the branches at the top of the tree. It became clear that the tree had grown so big at the top it became out of balance; the roots beneath the surface were too weak to withstand the weight of the tree and it had toppled over. But something had caused those roots to stop growing. As I looked closer, I could see that the roots had become separated from those that were still in the ground and they had a sort of decay all over them, which must have been the cause for their weakening. The decay had rotted the roots in the ground and the tree had become undernourished.

The tree reminded me of this passage. It reminded me that although it may appear on the outside that we are growing and becoming bigger and stronger, beneath the surface we just might be holding on to something that decays the root. Although Jesus promises us that He will tend to us, His branches, we still have a responsibility to hand over all the things to Him that are decaying our roots. This might mean that we have to do some digging around and ask for help, it may be messy and may unearth somethings we didn't know were there but that's what it means to be connected to the vine. He cleanses us from the inside out.

Is there anything that could be decaying your roots at the moment?

In verse 9 Jesus instructs us to continually let His love nourish our hearts. If we do, we will live empowered by His love, and the joy we experience will fill our hearts to overflowing with gladness. Isn't that beautiful? When we overflow with gladness it's impossible not to let that affect the world around us. We find as we accept His love for us, our love for others grows and we begin to *'love each other deeply'* just as He commands in verse 12.

Because we are all connected to the same vine the same life blood flows through us all. If we choose not to love one another our fellowship with the vine becomes severed. If we are attached to the vine, we are attached to His branches. Which means that we are all one in Him. Despite what we feel about one another, we are to live together in this picture of unity. Any disgruntlement or hurt He will, if allowed, gently prune and allow growth. Love produces love. An eye for an eye will only bring us a world full of blind people and that's not the mission we are on. Jesus says, 'For the greatest love of all is a love that sacrifices all. And this great love is demonstrated when a person sacrifices his life for his friends' (verse 13). I don't think Jesus is asking us here to die for our friends, but I do wonder.

What could we sacrifice in order to live in more unity?

In that last portion of the chapter Jesus is encouraging His disciples in that, despite the world hating them they have hope.

Because their allegiance is not to the world it's to Him and the divine helper will lead them, they have the ability to overcome that persecution. As do we. It might feel hard at times having to deal with our hearts and renounce the lies, but we have the love of the Father, the Son and the Holy Spirit and their wisdom will be enough. We have to choose our battles wisely and choose to war with the right weaponry. So, with this in mind:

Is there a battle you need to retreat from?

A Warning

Read John 16:1-33

Jesus has a warning for His disciples in this chapter regarding the trap of confusion and doubt. See, in times of confusion and moments where we wobble in faith we find that chaos begins to brew. In times of chaos it's not so easy to recognise what's happening in our hearts; these are the times that we can be caught off guard. Confusion and doubt are not from God. When we face issues in this world that come to confuse us and give us doubt in our hearts, these do not come from the Father, but these are things that we need to learn to navigate as we've discovered throughout these devotions.

We know that in life stuff just happens and we have to learn to hold on to our peace in amongst the world. But we also fight against the principalities and power of Satan who roams around looking for his chance to pounce. There are times when we fall prey to him. Maybe if we aren't looking after ourselves as well as we should be and are feeling particularly burnt out, we might fall in to overwhelm, which causes confusion and eventually doubt. This is why it's so important that we are careful when it comes to our daily schedules, eating, exercise and all the other responsibilities that come with taking care of ourselves. Thankfully, in verse 7 Jesus informs His disciples that, the Divine Encourager has been released to identify sin, prove to the world that God is righteous, and His judgements are good. Jesus has already won this battle and no matter what we face, the devil cannot win; he has already received his sentence!

The footnotes in The Passion Translation help to decipher what this all means. In essence, 'sin . . . righteousness . . . and judgement are related to three persons'. Sin is related to Adam, for it was through Adam that sin entered humanity:

When Adam sinned, the entire world was affected. Sin entered human experience, and death was the result. And so death followed this sin, casting its shadow over all humanity, because all have sinned. (Romans 5:12)

Righteousness is related to Christ, because it comes through Him, and He has become our righteousness:

For it is not from man that we draw our life but from God as we are being joined to Jesus, the Anointed One. And now he is our God-given wisdom, our virtue, our holiness, and our redemption. (1 Corinthians 1:30)

Judgement is related to Satan, for the pure works of Christ bring judgement to the works of Satan. If we do not embrace Christ's righteousness, we will share Satan's judgement.

No matter how bad we feel we must hold on to the One who set us free!

Where in your life is confusion and doubt?

Jesus goes on to explain in verse 13, 'But when the truth-giving Spirit comes, he will unveil the reality of every truth within you. He won't speak his own message, but only what he hears from the Father, and he will reveal prophetically to you what is to come.' The word 'truth' here in Greek is 'reality', not doctrine.

It is the application of the truth that matters, not the superficial knowledge.

I know many people who are very knowledgeable about the Word of God. They are great when it comes to teaching context and I love to learn from them. But it's useless knowing the history and the context if we aren't applying the message. I'm not saying here that these knowledgeable people don't apply the Word, but I am saying we can sometimes run the risk ourselves of not applying it. Especially the bits that challenge us. The Holy Spirit is our teacher, we receive conviction from Him. We receive instruction from the Father. If we aren't obedient to what He's telling us to do what do you think might happen?

My eldest son is a character. We were only laughing today about his desire to do just enough to get by. My middle son is a learner. He practises his spellings, reading and times tables at every given opportunity, but my eldest will do just enough to say he has done what has been asked of him. My middle son consistently passes his tests and my eldest gets just enough to not be marked down into a lower group. A while ago my eldest son had the opportunity to apply to be an ambassador in his class. He had to prepare a speech over the weekend to give to his class on Monday morning then they would vote for the best one. I helped him to write it then I told him, how often you practise it will determine the result you get. He practised every day and wrote it out three times to perfect it. This was something he really wanted to achieve. Monday came and he was the best speaker in his class, and he got the role. When I collected him from school that day I asked him what he had learned from that experience. He said that the results are determined by how hard you try. It's a lesson he learned all by himself, which will influence him as he continues to learn, he now knows that he needs to work at things he wants to achieve.

I believe that this is what Jesus means about our application of the Word. If we constantly read about faith and never step out in it, we will never experience the lessons. If we are reading about forgiveness but never extend it, how do we know about healing and restoration? We need to experience the Word as well as to know the Word.

Is there something you could be applying today?

As I read on about the pain the disciples would suffer as Jesus left them, I was drawn to the analogy of childbirth. Jesus speaks of the immense pain a woman goes through to give birth, which is short lived because of the wonderful joy she experiences to hold her newborn baby. It's true. When I had my first son I was traumatised. There was no way on this earth I would go through that ever again! Here I am eight years later with three boys. I did it again – twice! It's such a good example, though, of what we go through spiritually to become free. It's painful pulling things from our hearts and allowing God to deal with them. The final verse of this chapter tells us that everything Jesus teaches is so that we may have peace and confidence as we rest in Him. That's our bundle of joy after the painstaking ordeal of labour. I'd like to leave you this week with this question:

What does freedom and a life filled with peace look like to you?

What Jesus Wants

WEEK 39

Read John 17:1-26

How amazing is it that Jesus actually prays for us? I can never quite grasp that concept in my mind that He actually intercedes on our behalf! This next chapter is a picture of Him doing just that and it's filled with wisdom too.

How does it make you feel to know that Jesus prays for you?

In the first part of the prayer Jesus is proclaiming the work He has done. He came to show the people the splendour of God. He then goes on to pray for His disciples. As I was reading the first few verses, I was struck by verse 9. Jesus said:

So with deep love, I pray for my disciples. I'm not asking on behalf of the unbelieving world, but for those who belong to you, those you have given me.

It struck me because I was under the impression that Jesus loves the world. He died for the world, didn't He? But upon further reading I found the study notes by Brian Simmons in The Passion Translation to say this:

This is emphatic in the Greek sentence structure. How could it be that Jesus loves the world and gave himself for the sin of the world, yet emphasises that he is praying for his disciples and not praying for the world? Jesus' coming into the world brings life to those who believe and judgment to those who do not. The implication is that the key to reaching the world is the life, maturity, unity, and love of the disciples. This does not mean that Jesus doesn't love the world, but that the world will only be reached when the disciples come into the fullness of Christ and in unity of the faith. This is what consumes the heart of Jesus as he prays for them before the cross.

That's pretty amazing stuff. In order for the disciples to reach the world they needed maturity, unity and love. When they have this, they will come into the fullness of Christ and unity of the faith. This consumes the heart of Jesus, which tells us a lot about how He would like His church body to look.

How do we develop maturity so that we too can be united together in Christ?

As we continue to read on to the prayer Jesus prayers for us, He continues to talk of unity. He goes on to say:

I pray for them all to be joined together as one even as you and I, Father, are joined together as one. I pray for them to become one with us so that the world will recognise that you sent me. For the very glory you have given to me I have given them so that they will be joined together as one and experience the same unity that we enjoy. You live fully in me and now I live fully in them so that they will experience perfect unity, and the world will be convinced that you have sent me, for they will see that you love each one of them with the same passionate love that you have for me.

Unity comes with experiencing the glory of God together. As we work together as His body for His glory, we become one in Christ. I hear a lot spoken about unity in church and I'm not so sure we all agree on what that looks like, but I know that when we experience it, we will know what Christ means.

What do you think a mature, united community of love should look like?

Captured

WEEK 40

Read John 18:1-40

As we draw near to the end of John's Gospel, we find Jesus in the garden of Gethsemane where He would be captured after Judas turned Him over to the Pharisees and leading priests. These power-hungry men gave Judas up to 600 men that day to arrest Jesus. Can you imagine being faced with that amount of men? They knew all too well how powerful Jesus was and they weren't taking any chances.

As they approached, Jesus asked who it was they were looking for. They told Him, and as Jesus spoke the words 'I am He', the mob of men fell back! This wasn't a tripping over one another either, it was a move of God. I love the image of God here fighting for His beloved Son. He fights for us in the exact same way.

Although God's plan in this story was for His Son to be captured, I thought it would be a good time to reflect on how God fights for us with this image in mind.

I know that there have been times in my life where I've been victim to injustice. When I have tried in my own strength to fight against these circumstances it has never worked out well. I find when I'm fighting my own corner, I can become angry, bitter and resentful which in the long run results in defeat. The times that I've allowed God to go to work, He has never failed to show up. I've learnt over time that it's far better to take my heartache to God, be still and allow Him to move.

Is there something in your life that's wearing you down at the moment?

When Peter decides to fight an injustice, we see that also ends in suffering for him. This is exactly what happens when we respond to something in anger. Although we might not physically cut off the ear of the person we are angry at, our irate response could deafen their ear to the love God has for them. Not only that, the people who witness our behaviour fail to see the message Jesus brings through us, as they see our outburst. Peter responded in anger, yes, his motive was to protect Jesus, his beloved friend and Saviour, but Peter got in the way of God's plan.

There are times that we get in the way a lot too. Especially when we think we are protecting our loved ones. I'm a fixer. If there's something going on my natural response it to want to fix it and bring peace and order as quickly as I can. Because of this nature I can be known to carry another person's offence. I side with my loved one and the offending party then becomes a foe. This is not a Christlike response and neither is it something that will mirror His image to those around us.

How could you help people to let go of resentment when they've been hurt?

After Jesus cleaned up Peter's mess He was taken to go before Annas. As Peter was allowed through the gate, he was recognised by a servant girl which brought about His first denial of Jesus. Peter was scared, I imagine, and had no idea what was going on. He certainly had a change of heart; Jesus had predicted he would. I also believe that Peter would be feeling a little ashamed of his outburst. That's the trouble with angry reactions; it's always an opportunity for shame. Shame isn't something God wants us to carry.

Despite Peter's reaction to the soldier being wrong he needn't have felt shameful about it. Although it is a natural reaction and it's one the devil knows all too well, it never fails to sadden my heart when I see good people fall into the trap of shame. I was there once too; it severed many relationships in my life for many years. Thankfully, we serve a God of restoration so it's never the end of a relationship, there is always hope as we will see later on for Peter.

When I was 17 I moved out of my mum's house and in with a friend I'd met on my first day at high school when I was 11. We were the best of friends and extremely excited to be entering into this independence together. The excitement didn't last long. Within months we were being really mean to one another and patience was wearing thin for both of us; it ended in tears. Thankfully, over time our friendship was restored and I'm pleased to report that 21 years later we are still the best of friends. Did we do mean things to one another again? Yes – of course we did. Us humans are really unthoughtful at times. But time and time again our friendship has been restored because we love one another so much we see beyond the mistakes and forgive. When I became a Christian, my friend thought I was crackers. In fact, one of her fears was the church we had joined was some weird cult. But she supported me and came along to see us baptised and allowed me to talk to her about Jesus, even though I could see her jaw clench as I would begin to talk! Although the one thing she did say was that she noticed, as time went by, I became less and less angry.

The first Christian conference I went to, the preacher got on stage and introduced her childhood best friend. She talked about how much they had been through and that to serve in ministry with her was a true blessing. The theme of that conference was 'set her up to win'. I remember thinking how much I longed for my friend to be there with me. Later that night the preacher asked us to think of that one person who wasn't with us and asked that we pray for them. I wrote my friend's name on the card we were given and I cried out to God in my heart for her. This year I attended that same conference with my best friend! She met with Jesus that weekend and gave her heart to Him.

This story is the reason that shame is something that we need not carry. If I had held on to shame and ended my friendship with her she would never have seen the goodness of God. She wouldn't have seen the transformation in me and she wouldn't have experienced it for herself. The ability to forgive and detach from anger, bitterness and resentment is crucial to restoration and redemption. If we find that we are still feeling the need to hide away from social circles or communities, we might have been contained or captured by shame. Is there someone or something you need to forgive?

Have you been captured by shame?

In relating this chapter to the experiences we may suffer my intention is not to take away the suffering that Jesus experienced in the garden of Gethsemane and beyond. It is to expand the freedom that we have because of His suffering. Because He took those brutal beatings, was ridiculed and shamed for us, we have freedom. That freedom comes with a responsibility to live as best we can in His image. So, I encourage you today to go through the questions served in these pages with the help of the Holy Spirit and deal with all things that distance you from the life He died for you to have.

Flogged

WEEK 41

Read John 19:1-17

This is by far the most heart-breaking chapter of the Bible. Although, as we will read next week, Jesus was crucified, this part of His sacrifice was the most torturous. The length of time that Jesus endured this painstaking experience isn't mentioned, but the description of the weapon used is enough to imagine the ordeal. The weapon was a large leather whip with at least three strands, each embedded with sharpened pieces of bone and metal, designed to lacerate the skin. The weighted strands would strike the skin so violently that it would break open immediately, cutting through the muscle to the bone. Historians have said that this alone was a form of execution and many who endured this pain would not have survived.

This punishment was also known as 'scourging', and it was a punishment that was deliberately humiliating. It was so demeaning that it is said to have not been one that Romans would endure; it was a punishment only fit for a slave, or non-Romans who were considered lesser to the Roman group. To make it even more degrading it would be carried out in the public eye; the victim would be naked and bound to a post or frame and beaten from the shoulders to the loins. Jesus was left bloody, weak and in the most excruciating pain.

The reason that this awful chastisement took place was because Pilate could not make up his mind what to do with Jesus. He didn't really know what charge to hold against Him, but it was in Pilate's interest to keep the peace in the region. He thought that by humiliating Jesus by flogging and presenting Him in the mock robe with His crown of thorns that the crowd would be satisfied. But he was very much mistaken.

How does it make you feel to know that Jesus endured this pain for you?

Pilate did not want to be responsible for giving the death sentence to Jesus and he had hoped that by torturing Him so terribly the religious sect and the people would have been satisfied. As we know, they weren't. The Jewish leaders inform Pilate that the charge is blasphemy, going against this law:

Anyone who blasphemes the Name of the LORD must be stoned to death by the whole community of Israel. Any native-born Israelite or foreigner among you who blasphemes the Name of the LORD must be put to death. (Leviticus 24:16 NLT)

When Pilate heard this, he was deeply alarmed. The Aramaic can be translated as 'his soul collapsed' because he knew that at this point he had no alternative but to send Jesus to the cross. I find it fascinating that following the ordeal Jesus had endured He barely spoke. Unless it was to speak the truth.

But what I find even more fascinating is that the group of people only days before shouting 'Hosanna', which means 'Lord save us', are now shouting 'Crucify Him!' Why was there such a change of heart? What we don't envisage in the descriptions of the text here is the war that is going on in the spiritual realm. We saw in the chapter regarding Judas taking the bread from

Jesus that in that moment Satan entered his heart. Here we see a group of people who are working for the same enemy. They don't know it, but these people are being used as foot soldiers for the devil. He thinks that this pain and suffering will result in his defeat. Thankfully we know different. The defeat belongs to Jesus. He will ALWAYS fight for us.

As followers of Jesus we, too, are fighting continually a spiritual battle and there will be times when the people around us are ignorant to being used as foot soldiers for the opposition. We need to be aware at all times that this battle was already won in light of what we read in these chapters.

How can you remind yourself that Jesus is always fighting for you?

Have you ever been in a situation where you can't do right nor wrong? This is where Pilate was. He did not want to kill Jesus but he had a reputation to uphold and a status to maintain. It wasn't a situation that was going to go well. The Jewish authorities turned to blackmail in verse 12; they reminded Pilate that not going through with the death penalty for Jesus would end in ruin for his career. They gave him no choice.

Let us think for a moment what that might look like in the world. This man of authority is placing a career decision based on the life of the Saviour of the world. I know that in reality this is never a literal decision we will have to make, but there are compromises we have to make as we learn to navigate life and follow Jesus. If we want to be His disciple and bring glory to His name, there are some decisions that we will have to make that don't fit in with the people around us.

My husband and I own a property management company and we work with lots of people who invest in properties. It's not huge and we don't earn lots of money, contrary to what some may think. We earn enough to get by. There have been opportunities given to us that could have meant we earned more money, but we have had to decline those opportunities because we know that they would not glorify Jesus. If we are invited to manage a property for a client and it is not up to the legal standard for rent then we will ask the client to make it so; if they refuse then we will not work with them. It's as simple as that. We won't ever get rich by doing this, but we will bring glory to our Lord and Saviour.

There may be things in your life that you've had to turn away from because you know that they aren't honouring to God or maybe you haven't thought about it. But I would encourage you to evaluate the decisions that you make and their implications to your eternal inheritance because we are here to serve Jesus. He's the One who gave it all for us.

Are there some things in your life you need to reassess in light of this?

It is Finished

WEEK 42

Read John 19:17-42

Jesus was made to carry His cross along with two other men. He was mounted upon it, still wearing His thorn crown, a sign written in Aramaic, Latin and Greek placed above His head saying, 'Jesus of Nazareth, the King of the Jews'. There was even controversy over the sign, but Pilate stuck with it.

While they were waiting for Jesus to take His last breaths the soldiers were casting lots over Jesus' clothes. But because His tunic was seamless it was classed as one garment. The tunic was an emblem that gave reference to His pureness and holiness, the righteousness of the One from above. Because we now believe in Jesus, the One from above, that garment actually belongs to us. We are robed in His righteousness and holiness!

How does that make you feel?

When I read verse 25, I feel myself well up. I'm a mother and to read of Mary standing at the foot of the cross watching her young boy suffer, it breaks my heart. I can't begin to imagine what she was going through. Mary would have been around 50 years old and she was widowed. Jesus, her firstborn, was leaving her and she was watching this pain and suffering whilst soldiers gambled for His clothes. How painful that must have been.

Jesus looked down to see His beloved mother, John and the others and He spoke. He didn't speak many times on the cross – I'd imagine it would have been too painful to do so.

According to the accounts that I've read regarding crucifixion, every breath He took would have been painful without the injuries He had from being beaten. But despite that pain, His concern was for His beloved mother to be looked after and John, the disciple that had stood with Him through it all, was the one to do so. John always refers to Himself in the gospel as 'the one who Jesus loved', and we can see why. He didn't run, he stood with Jesus and for Jesus through all of the persecution, pain and suffering. Which is what we as disciples of Christ should do too: stand strong.

If there are times in your life when you feel you want to give up on Jesus, this is the chapter to read to remind yourself of why you are to stand strong. No matter how tough things get for me, whenever I reflect on what Jesus went through to save me from the clasp of Satan's hand, I know I can keep going: I can forgive the inexcusable, I can love the unlovable and I can do the undoable. Because He is strong, I am no longer weak. I can do all things through Christ who strengthens me.

What can you take from this chapter to help you stand strong?

As Jesus' fleshly life draws to a close, The Passion Translation footnotes explain that He fulfils yet another prophecy and speaks, 'I am thirsty.' The soldiers extend a significant hyssop branch that was used to paint the Passover blood on doorposts and used to cleanse lepers; the branch that would cleanse our souls was being used to give our Saviour the sour wine. He took the wine and with His last breath said, 'It is finished.'

Because Jesus had died before the two men either side of Him the soldiers did not break His legs, again a fulfilled prophecy. One of the soldiers did decide, though, to pierce His side; the water and blood that came from Jesus was significant to our new life. The water of the Spirit and blood of Jesus cleanses us, but Brian Simmons explains further in the footnotes to The Passion Translation about birth. When a child is born, he or she is born of blood and water. The significance of the blood and water here is our birth. The birth of His children, His followers, His disciples. We are His creation. Born to bring glory to the world by carrying within us His Spirit. How beautiful is that?

Although this is a deep and heart-breaking chapter, it is one to rejoice in because of what it means for us. Jesus overcame the world when He took His last breath. Everything Satan thought he was winning with was actually used against him to raise up an army. That army is you and I; we are the foot soldiers that Jesus chose to continue to take that message to the ends of the earth. I know that some days you might not feel that way, but it's the truth irrespective to how you feel. So in light of all this:

What could you do in the knowledge of being a chosen foot soldier of Jesus?

Nicodemus, despite hiding his faith in Jesus, knew that he was a foot soldier of Christ too. I love that in the end of this chapter he goes with Joseph to prepare Jesus and lay Him to rest. Or so they think.

Vanished

WEEK 43

Read John 20:1-18

How amazing is it that it was a group of women who discovered the empty tomb? I love it. I had a conversation with someone a while ago that was about women being ordained and whether or not they should be in leadership. I have to say leadership is a term I dislike in church, for some reason people seem to place those in leadership on a pedestal. The term itself means that you lead people. If you have ever influenced someone to make a decision, known to you or not, then you are a leader.

This particular day Mary was a leader. She led those with her to the tomb and she led Peter and John in telling them what she had seen. The woman at the well led all the people in her village to Jesus . . . I could go on, but I won't. The point I'm making here is irrespective of age, gender or race we are all leaders. I'm sure that if you think about it you can name occasions when you have led others to do, think or shift perspective on something, we are always leading people conscious of doing so or not.

Can you name a time when you've influenced someone recently?

Verse 3 and 4 make me chuckle. Peter and John are so competitive! I love how John always calls himself the one who

Jesus loves, it's like he's making a huge statement to the world, isn't it? He's so confident in Jesus' love for him. But let's not take away from him that he was the only one with Mary standing with Jesus through all of the suffering. Peter denied Him and would still be carrying that shame. I imagine Peter was in a very dark place at this time and was desperate to see Jesus to apologise. But all the same, their cycle of competing is very evident throughout this book.

We see a lot of competition in the world today too. The irony of this is people in church more so than the world, are fighting for the same thing most of the time. The mentality is that there isn't enough room for two people who have a heart for the same vision. Which is ridiculous when you think about the unique abilities that God has given to each of us. We are each called to play a different part of the same body, just because my heart is for women to discover their identity in Him doesn't mean to say there isn't room for someone else with that vision too.

My husband and I went through a process a couple of years ago called Myers Briggs. It's a personality test that helps you to discover a little more about who you are. The results showed that we were complete opposites in every way other than being extroverts, which is really tough when you are in our company because we are both fighting to be heard! For years prior to doing this test we struggled to work together, which was a nightmare because as well as sharing children and a home, we have a business together. But when we discovered how our opposite abilities complement one another we realised that actually we can work really, really well together. If we were football players, I would be a striker and he would be a defender. The team needs both to win a game. This is the same in church or workplaces. Just because two or more people have the same goal it doesn't mean to say that they have to work against one another to succeed.

If we find ourselves feeling insecure by another person, I'd say that we are being deceived. Because if we are secure in our identity in Christ then we wouldn't need to compare and compete with others. Comparison is a trap, it's something that will have you coveting what others have in no time, and whilst we are looking on other people's gifts with envy, we are not being thankful for the those that God gave us. John was confident in who he was in Jesus' eyes. Because of that he stood firm and was by His side through it all. Peter was robbed of his identity and ran and because of that he resented John. Let us not be caught in the comparison trap. We need to keep our hearts set on who God says we are. If we are confident in that we will then be able to see that those around us are gifted too, we will be able to complement one another and bring glory to Jesus' wonderful name.

Who does God say you are?

Mary then enters the tomb to see that Jesus is gone. In those days grave robbery wasn't uncommon so I'm guessing that was Mary's first speculation. Through the tears she could barely see when the angels spoke to her – well that's my assumption. It's clear with her turning to leave, her only concern was where Jesus was, so much so that she completely neglected two angels. Maybe they looked like normal people and she didn't recognise them to be angelic, we don't know. Then, blurry eyed, she saw a man at the entrance to the tomb whom she thought was a gardener. It wasn't until the man spoke her name that she realised it was Jesus. I imagine she'd heard Him call her name so many times before she just knew at the tone in His voice it was Him. Maybe because Jesus looked different that day she didn't recognise Him, we don't know, but by His voice she knew Him. Which is what He had previously taught them.

We then revert back to the beginning of this story as Jesus instructs her to go tell the others His message. A woman. Instructed to take a message from the Lord to other men and women. Who'd have thought it?!

I believe that we are all called and chosen to take Jesus' message to people no matter what our gender, age or race. There have been many times my children have spoken something from God into my life. I could have smiled and dismissed it because of their age, but I don't believe that's what God wants. He wants us to remain humble, have a teachable heart and allow those around us to be used by Him. We are all on an equal playing field and He shows no favouritism to people. There's a firmly planted desire in each of our hearts to glorify Jesus using our talents, treasure and time so I want to ask you:

What's your desire?

I'm going to cheat and add a question in to this devotional as we are nearing the end:

What is it you are doing about that desire in your heart?

Maybe you're sitting on it thinking that it's not something you can achieve, maybe you are waiting for the right timing, maybe you are struggling with comparison and see many people around you who are better equipped. Wherever you are at the moment, I want to encourage you to do something to put a step towards seeing the desire in your heart become a reality in your life. God is with you and He is rooting for you too. Don't allow it to vanish.

The Breath of Life

WEEK 44

Read John 20:19-31

How remarkable to have been in the house with the disciples the day that Jesus entered through a locked door. Imagine the scene. They are all scared stiff and hiding from the Roman authorities, as they are believed to have taken Jesus' body. They are locked in a secret room and Jesus appears. How wonderful is that?

I know myself that in times where I've been too paralysed to move, I've spent time in my secret place with Jesus. Calling out to Him asking for Him to come and make sense of the situation I'm in. I can tell you that He has never failed to come when I've called. No matter what the situation I know that Jesus will come and breathe life into me as He did the disciples this day.

The description in verse 22 of Jesus breathing into the disciples does not appear anywhere else in the New Testament according to The Passion Translation footnotes. It is the same word used when God breathed the breath of life into Adam's nostrils in Genesis 2:7. This was a new beginning for the disciples and new life with His breath in their lungs.

I don't know what you believe about being baptised in the Holy Spirit or if you do. But I do. I believe it because that's what happened to me. I talked about my experience of first coming to know Jesus in the beginning of this devotional and it was most certainly a supernatural experience. I remember after only a few short weeks of attending church standing in worship and crying out to Jesus in my heart to come and change my life. I was in that row filled with shame and feeling utterly worthless. My heart's cry was, 'Jesus, if you are there, I need you. Come and show me how I'm meant to live because I can't do this anymore.' In that moment the minister and another lady came and prayed with me. As I sobbed uncontrollably, the Holy Spirit fell upon me and did something that I can only describe as beautiful. I felt totally different after that day. The scriptures became alive to me as I read them, I felt I had supernatural wisdom and I believed in my heart that Jesus Christ is the true Saviour the Bible tells us about. I knew that my life was beginning again with a whole new perspective. The key to this beautiful encounter was my posture that day. It was one of surrender. I knew that I had nothing left in me to give, I had literally given up on myself and my only desire was to know Jesus. We have to want Jesus to work in our hearts. It's not easy to let go and allow Him complete control though. Although to the world this day it could look like I broke down and gave up, I didn't. I was built up and given life by the only One who could offer life in its fullness. I was filled with His Spirit and given a new start.

Have you ever encountered Jesus in this way?

The reason that I know Jesus wants us all to experience this is because of what we read in the next verse. He wants us to take His goodness to the world and in order to do that we need to be FULL of Him. Jesus was equipping His disciples to take this message to the world, they needed to be full of Him and emptied of themselves. Because of this new life He gave to them we know Jesus today. They were filled with courage to keep on proclaiming His goodness, which thousands of years later reached me and you. It's now our job to do the same so that in thousands of years from now someone like me knows the truth.

From the minute I received the Holy Spirit I had wisdom I'd never experienced before and boldness to speak about it too. Now, please don't think I'm being egotistical here, I'm not. But I seem to have the ability by the power of the Holy Spirit to speak the right things at the right times to people. This is certainly not a natural ability of mine. Anyone who knows me well will know that quite often in my natural strength I put my foot in it, so to speak. I often speak without thinking and have been known to say some ridiculous things! But by the prompting of the Holy Spirit I don't. It's a gift and one that Jesus wants us all to have.

How would having this wisdom impact your life and the lives of those around you?

As we read in the next portion, Thomas has missed out and he doesn't believe the disciples have had that experience. He states that he needs to see Jesus to believe it. Thomas is nicknamed 'The Doubter' a lot when we read about him. We don't see him speak much, but when we do it's always to question something. I don't think that by his questioning he should be called a doubter. Jesus proves here that He welcomes our doubts as an opportunity to show His goodness. In any relationship we have questions that need to be asked so why would this one be any different?

Jesus tells Thomas that those who believe in their hearts without seeing Him will be blessed even more. He's talking about us here. When we know that Jesus is who He says He is without ever actually seeing Him we are even more blessed than those who stood before Him that day. I think I can understand that to be the experiences I've talked about throughout this book. I've experienced such goodness from a man that I've never physically seen and that sets my heart on fire. This man is more real to me than anyone I have ever seen with my eyes and that's what keeps me going. I don't see Him, yet I have some of my most meaningful conversations with Him. My eyes don't see a physical being, yet my heart is filled with His presence. My home is filled with His presence, my car and my workplace too. Isn't that amazing?

Jesus came so that we might have life in abundance, and we have the opportunity to be filled with His breath and proclaim this goodness to the ends of the earth! He chose YOU. He wants to fill you with His wonderful presence so that each and every person you encounter feels His presence too. You are precious to Him and so are all the people you see every single day. No matter who they are, He wants them to be filled too. It's our job to take that message with us everywhere we go. With this in mind let me ask you for the last question of the day?

How full are you at the minute?

It maybe that you answer that question with a 'not very'. If that is the case let me encourage you to find a secret room, lock yourself away and ask Jesus to come and show you His goodness. Take your surrender posture and sit until you feel Him come and breathe life into you. He wants to, the question is, how much do you want Him to?

Restored

WEEK 45

Read John 21:1-25

Here we see Peter decide to go back to what he knows best: fishing. Although it's not written in this account of John, Luke 24:49 explains that Jesus told them to wait. Peter is being disobedient in turning back to his old life. Not only that, he's taking some others with him.

I think I can empathise with Peter here though. He's denied Jesus and he is thinking that the life he had while his beloved teacher walked with him is over. So, it's time to go back to life as he once knew it. I can imagine that Peter felt really dejected at this time. I can place myself in his shoes because I know the feeling all too well. There have been many times on this journey that I've thought about going back to how I was before.

I can't tell you how many times I've wanted to give up on things that I feel Jesus has told me to do. This book is a perfect example. In 2015 I felt God prompting me to write. It's now 2019 and it's taken four years for me to get these words on paper and learn a whole lot of lessons. I started this a year ago and there have been so many times I've shut my laptop down and decided to go back to spending my evenings watching Netflix instead! There are many other examples I can give to you too – I'm not a very good finisher. I like to start things and never really seem to see them through to the end, so to have got to the last week, I'm feeling pretty good right now. It hasn't been without its battles though. The same thoughts go over and over in my mind: I'm not good enough, I never finish anything, I'm not a writer, what if it's rubbish? If I allow these thoughts to consume me I will become overwhelmed and in a state of paralysis; I'll end up filled with a lack of self-worth and give up. I think that this is what happened to Peter.

Has there been a time in your life you've wanted to turn back?

The disciples were in the boat that day catching nothing at all. They had turned away from Jesus to catch fish, but the fact is without Him we won't be catching anything. It is His Holy Spirit that fills us with strength to carry on. No matter how absurd we think the instruction is, it is only in our obedience that Jesus will allow us to see a miracle.

Jesus appears on the shore and calls out to them to cast their nets on the other side of the boat, something that Peter may have thought ridiculous but in his obedience we see Jesus' miracle.

This book has been a true blessing for me to write and I've learnt so much about Jesus and how He works through me along the way. I've put my faith in Him to give me the words of wisdom to write as well as the finance to publish. I'm not there yet, but in faith I'm hoping that you will be reading it. If you are, there's another miracle that Jesus accomplished.

When Jesus called out to the disciples it was John who recognised His voice. This wouldn't have done much good to the comparison trap Peter found himself in. I'd imagine Peter full of sorrow at his rejection of the Messiah whilst going about his business, which may have been the reason he didn't recognise Jesus' voice. When we ponder the disappointment, dejection and doubt it hinders our ability to hear Jesus too. As soon as

John announces that it's Jesus, we see Peter take to the water to reach Him.

What do you need to do in obedience then put your faith into in order to see a miracle?

The large catch that day was significant to Peter, the first time he encountered Jesus he had the same experience. Jesus was inviting him again to follow Him and become a fisher of men. The catch resembles the harvest of the nations that will come to Jesus through the work of the disciples. I do wonder if they knew the significance of this miracle. It's certainly something that would excite me.

During breakfast Jesus asks Peter if he burns with love for Him. This is something that is paramount to our journey. If we have a burning desire in our heart for Jesus, then it's something He can work with. When Jesus asks, 'Do you love me more than these?' He could have been referring to the fish as Peter really did love to fish, or it could be towards the disciples. Peter had always boasted that he loved Jesus so much he would die for Him, although when push came to shove Peter rejected Him. Jesus asks Peter three times if he loves Him, the same amount that Peter denied Jesus. This is a beautiful picture of His heart for restoration when we mess up. No matter what we do, Jesus' heart is for us to be restored to the place He called us to. Peter was the rock on whom He would build His church; here Jesus was reminding Peter of that.

Upon his restoration Peter's eyes immediately stray to John. His concern, what will Jesus do with him. Jesus responds, 'If I decide to let him live until I return, what concern is that of yours? You must still keep on following Me!' I love that despite the instruction Jesus has just given to Peter he still wants to know what's happening to his competitor, John. That jealousy still seems to be there. I think that we will always struggle with comparison of others in our walk with Jesus, but we need not allow it to pull us away from our calling.

Jesus tells Peter that it is none of his business what John is called to do, as should it be with us when we have our eyes on others. All Peter needed to do was rest in what he had been instructed to do. As we read on through the Bible, we see that he does. But it's a lesson for us too. We must keep our eyes firmly fixed on the instructions we are each given individually.

What is Jesus instructing you to do?

This chapter is a beautiful picture of the restoration that Jesus wants to give to each of us, but we have to be willing to listen and apply His instruction.

I can't believe that we have now come to the end of the devotional. My prayer is that through it you have gained more knowledge of Jesus and who you are because of Him. His love for you is something that you can never, ever lose and if you allow Him, He will do some mighty things through you. Let us not feel stuck in a trap but let us live the life He died to give us. He loves us all because He loves us each.

Acknowledgements

I'm so honoured to have been given the words to write this book by God, so my first gratitude goes to Him. I am also thankful for all the people He placed around me to make this happen and would like to express my sincere thanks to them too. Because of you all, this God-given dream has become a reality.

Richard, my dear husband. God knew what He was doing when He placed us together. Your loving and giving nature continues to bless me. You have pushed me and encouraged me to do this and I thank you from the bottom of my heart. I'm honoured to be your wife and excited for all we will do in this lifetime together.

Kyan, Joel and Theo, my beautiful boys, your hearts are so big and minds so wise. You inspire me every day and I'm thankful to God for you all. I'm excited and expectant to see what you do on this earth. I know it's going to be an awesome journey.

Hayley, my beautiful God-given friend. After all these years God placed you back in my life. What a journey we have been on! I'm so thankful for working with you on this project, your hours of prayer, encouragement and editing. Your comfort and love. You've been such an inspiration, thank you.

The wonderful Renew ladies, each and every week you continue to encourage, pray and teach me. You were the first ever people to experience this study and I thank you all so much for being so open. Each of you allowed God to speak to your hearts and learnt so much from Him in this process. Thank you for sharing your highs and lows with me and being the amazing women of God that you are.

My first ever pastor, Lan. You led me to Jesus, you prayed for me, you encouraged me, you taught me what it was to be a disciple. You spent hours and hours with me and my family. I'm so thankful to you for this foundational teaching that has enabled me to join hands with Jesus and turn my back on fear and doubt. Thank you, Lan, you are a true inspiration.

Everyone who has prayed, given and encouraged me through this project – thank you! Your generosity has been mind-blowing. I can't believe how many people have supported me and given to make this happen. I'm blessed beyond words by all of you.

I can't wait to see what God will do with these pages. I'm expectant and excited to see many people hear His voice as they study His word and invite the Holy Spirit to speak to them directly.

Rach xx